Praise for

Building the Christian Family You Never Had

"Mary DeMuth offers positive encouragement and practical help for parents who want to do things a little differently than what they experienced growing up. *Building the Christian Family You Never Had* offers a fresh start and bright hope as you seek to raise godly children."

—KAROL LADD, author of *The Power of a Positive Mom*

"You are not alone as a pioneer parent who is blazing a new trail on the parenting journey. If you have longed for someone to show you how to build a family that is different from the family you grew up in, this book is for you!"

—JILL SAVAGE, executive director of Hearts at Home and
author of *Professionalizing Motherhood*

"As Mary shares her haunting story of a broken childhood, she provides a road map for breaking the cycle of family dysfunction. Her road map provides hope, courage, and grace, allowing any reader to walk with her on the continuing journey to wholeness."

—TIM RITER, professor at Azusa Pacific University and author of
Twelve Lies Husbands Tell Their Wives

"If your parents raised you in the 'old country,' you may wonder how to ground your kids in new soil. Mary DeMuth's insights about parenting—as well as life in general—will help you raise firmly planted, emotionally secure Christ-following kids."

—SANDRA L. GLAHN, adjunct professor at Dallas Theological Seminary
and coauthor of *Sexual Intimacy in Marriage* and *When Empty
Arms Become a Heavy Burden*

"This is an honest, thought-provoking, and life-changing book. If you want to parent differently than you were parented, this is a must-read!"

—MARY BYERS, author of *The Mother Load* and *How
to Say No...and Live to Tell About It*

"Mary DeMuth creates a compelling picture of what a Christian family should look like for those of us who never had one or may have never even seen one up close. Reading this book will change the way you think about love, parenting, and healing—and God's hope and plan for your life and the lives of your children."

—MICHAEL WARREN, executive story consultant on *Happy Days* and
co-creator and executive producer of *Step by Step* and *Family Matters*

"Mary adeptly encourages pioneer parents to seek healing for the pain and dysfunction they experienced during their formative years, while honoring their parents for the good they provided. Learning parents should study this volume with an open mind and an open heart."

—PAUL PETTIT, president of Dynamic Dads and author
of *Congratulations! You're Gonna Be a Dad!*

"*Building the Christian Family You Never Had* is for parents who have experienced some dysfunction (and which of us hasn't) but who also want to get past that dysfunction and raise emotionally and spiritually healthy children. Mary points us to principles deeply rooted in God's Word that apply the salve of truth mixed with grace, mercy, and hope."

—LINUS MORRIS, president of Christian Associates International

"Mary gives families a biblical blueprint for success without presenting her family as a perfect role model. I have many friends who did not grow up in a Christian home, and I would give them Mary's book in a second!"

—DENA DYER, author of *Grace for the Race: Meditations
for Busy Moms*

"In a refreshing voice and with wisdom and sensitivity, Mary DeMuth delivers a powerful message of liberty for all who want to break free from generational pain in order to parent in newness of life in Christ."

—JAN WINEBRENNER, author of *The Grace of Catastrophe* and
Intimate Faith

Building the Christian Family

You Never Had

A Practical Guide for Pioneer Parents

Mary E. DeMuth

WATERBROOK
PRESS

BUILDING THE CHRISTIAN FAMILY YOU NEVER HAD
PUBLISHED BY WATERBROOK PRESS
12265 Oracle Boulevard, Suite 200
Colorado Springs, Colorado 80921

All Scripture quotations, unless otherwise indicated, are taken from the *Holy Bible, New International Version®*. NIV®. Copyright © 1973, 1978, 1984 by International Bible Society. Used by permission of Zondervan Publishing House. All rights reserved. Scripture quotations marked (MSG) are taken from *The Message*. Copyright © 1993, 1994, 1995, 1996, 2000, 2001, 2002. Used by permission of NavPress Publishing Group. Scripture quotations marked (NASB) are taken from the *New American Standard Bible®* (NASB). © Copyright The Lockman Foundation 1960, 1962, 1963, 1968, 1971, 1972, 1973, 1975, 1977, 1995. Used by permission. (www.Lockman.org). Scripture quotations marked (NET) are taken from the *NET Bible,* copyright © 1996–2005 by Biblical Studies Press, LLC, www.bible.org. All rights reserved.

Italics in Scripture quotations reflect the author's added emphasis.

Details in some anecdotes and stories have been changed to protect the identities of the persons involved.

ISBN 978-1-4000-7031-2

Published in association with the literary agency of Alive Communications, Inc., 7680 Goddard Street, Suite 200, Colorado Springs, CO 80920, www.alivecommunications.com.

Published in the United States by WaterBrook Multnomah, an imprint of the Crown Publishing Group, a division of Random House Inc., New York.

WATERBROOK and its deer colophon are registered trademarks of Random House, Inc.

Library of Congress Cataloging-in-Publication Data
DeMuth, Mary E., 1967–
  Building the Christian family you never had : a practical guide for pioneer parents / Mary E. DeMuth.—1st ed.
    p. cm.
  Includes bibliographical references (pp. 199–207)
  ISBN 1-4000-7031-7
  1. Family—Religious aspects—Christianity. 2. Family—Religious life. I. Title.
BT707.7.D46 2006
248.8'.45—dc22

                                                    2005021095

Printed in the United States of America
2012

10 9 8 7 6 5 4 3 2

To Patrick, who holds my hand in the journey

Contents

Part I: Healing for the Past

Part II: God Is with You Today

viii   Contents

"Oops, We Did It Again" 118
      Forgiving Yourself; Forgiving Your Children
13   "But What If I Messed Up?" 126
      Using Your Past Sins to Teach Your Kids
14   "A Funny Thing Happened While Raising My Kids" 134
      Adding the Missing Ingredient—Laughter
15   "Why Can't I Go to Grandpa's House?" 141
      Protecting Your Children While Preserving the Relationship
16   "Someone, Please Help Us!" 149
      Finding a Mentor

Part III: Hope for the Future

17   "I Can't Wipe the Wilderness Off My Shoes" 159
      Integrating God's Promised-Land Principle
18   "The Wolves Are Howling" 169
      Preparing Your Children for the Big, Bad World
19   "We're in This Together" 178
      Encouraging Other Pioneer Parents
20   "What Now?" 184
      Parenting with an Eternal Perspective

Discussion Guide: Questions for Reflection and Growth 190
Appendix: Helpful Resources 199
Notes 203

Acknowledgments

Thank you, Patrick, for walking this marriage and parenting journey with me. Your consistent and persistent love is my backbone. Thank you, Sophie, Aidan, and Julia, for the privilege and joy of being your mom.

Thanks, Chip, for embracing this book idea the moment I shared it. Your persistence in convincing me to be a "parenting expert" worked, although I still feel quite inadequate for the title. Beth, thanks for taking the agenting baton and sprinting with it.

I couldn't have written this book without the inexhaustible help of my critique team, Life Sentence. Leslie, D'Ann, and Suzanne—your insights, vision, and encouragement made this a better book. Suzanne, I am particularly thankful for the sacrifice of love you made to ready this book for publication.

Sandi, thanks for mentoring me through this maze of publication. But more than that, thank you for your amazing friendship.

Thank you, prayer team, for faithfully praying me through this book: Kevin and Renee Bailey, Gahlen and LeeAnn Crawford, Eric and Katy Gedney, Kim Griffith, Ed and Sue Harrell, Diane and Jessica Klapper, Susanne Maynes, Hud and Nancy McWilliams, Renee and Michael Mills, Kathy O'Neill, Catalin and Shannon Popa, Tom and Holly Schmidt, Mike and Heidi Van Dyken, J. R. and Ginger Vassar, Rod and Mary Vestal, Jodie Westfall, and Liz Wolf. If any person is touched by the message of this book, it is due to God's grace and your faithfulness in praying for me.

Thanks to the faithful folks at WaterBrook Press. Ron Lee, you were a terrific editor to work with. Your direction and gentle guidance made the manuscript sing.

Don Pape, it's a privilege to call you friend.

Thank you, Mom, for being brave enough to read this book. I love you.

Jesus, you are my strength when I'm weak, my joy when I'm weeping, my hope when I doubt. Thanks for looking under the hemlock tree, lifting my head, and bringing me home.

Preface

For Us, Parenting Is Uncharted Territory

If you cannot get rid of the family skeleton,
you may as well make it dance.
—George Bernard Shaw

Forging new paths for our children, grandchildren, and their grandchildren is a holy and joyful occupation that delivers eternal rewards. But when you are a first-generation Christian, it is a parenting journey fraught with obstacles. As a pioneer parent, you don't have a map to guide you as you forge a completely new path for later generations to follow.

Pioneer parents are people who grew up in homes they don't want to duplicate. They are folks who may not relate to the advice given by parenting experts who grew up in stable homes. One pioneer parent expressed this sentiment: "I'm sick and tired of parenting books written by someone who became a Christian at age three. Where are the books written for *me?*" There are millions of Christian parents who grew up without Christian parents. Today they are struggling to instill Christian values in their children without having seen such values modeled in their childhood homes.

There are others with slightly different stories. They may have grown up in what was touted as a Christian home but were never exposed to a consistent, biblical model of the life of faith. As children, they may have heard about what was proper while they watched their parents violate what was taught. Others may have grown up in religious homes where rage and chaos reigned. Those who were raised in such homes are pioneers because they, too, want to break the cycle of dysfunction that influenced their upbringings.

As pioneer parents, we're like researchers, trying many different ways to solve life-impacting problems. Our parenting is characterized by inquiry, experimentation, observation. Often we fail. But sometimes we stumble upon something that works, and we build on that success.

Because we are first-generation Christians raising children in a new way, we are on a maiden voyage, taking a journey into what is largely unknown to us. The word *pioneer* connotes an initiation, a new beginning. Every day, raising our children is a mission of discovery. We may have vague connections to our old way of life, but in order to produce a genesis generation, we have to initiate a new method of family building. As pioneer parents, we have to do work that bewilders us, work that keeps us up at night. But it also is work that brings us great joy.

PIONEERS ARE INNOVATORS

I grew up reading and watching *Little House on the Prairie*. I secretly longed to be Mary, the "good girl" pioneer clad in a calico-print dress with matching bonnet, who followed her Pa to new places and adventures. When I first thought of the pioneering metaphor for this book, my mind raced back to those who dared to venture dusty trails into the great wide unknown. I realize, though, that pioneering in terms of prairies and wagon trains is foreign to most people, so I prefer to think of pioneers in a more "scientific" sense. Pioneers are the people on the cutting edge of research, innovation, and discovery. They may not be populating new lands, but they discover technologies and remedies vital to our daily lives.

Consider the similarities between scientific innovators and pioneer parents:

1. We face criticism. In the mid-1980s, Dr. Robin Warren and Dr. Barry Marshall faced stinging criticism from their colleagues when they dared to suggest that bacteria caused most ulcers. Even after initial tests proved their theory correct, the mainstream medical community ridiculed them. In the same way, pioneer parents often face criticism from those closest to them—their own parents. Criticism, unfortunately, is a sad inevitability for most pioneer parents. But it's something we can navigate, as we will discover in the chapters that follow.

2. We fail—and try again. Every facet of science involves experimentation. Trial and error. Lots of failure before the big breakthrough. Thomas Edison once stated, "I have not failed. I've just found ten thousand ways that don't work."

Peptic ulcers were fairly common but rarely cured. According to common belief, stress and diet caused these ulcers. Still, Warren and Marshall spent *years* trying to prove their theory that bacteria could be the cause. They experimented by examining tissue samples taken from people with peptic ulcers.

Since pioneer parents also are breaking new ground, they parent by trial and error. But they don't allow failure to deter them. With the tenacity of scientists on the brink of discovery, they continue on because they want their children to grow up in a stable, loving home.

3. We get lonely. Warren and Marshall not only experienced the ridicule of the scientific community, but they became isolated from their colleagues when their promising findings were dismissed. Similarly, pioneer parenting brings its own sense of isolation. Those who were not parented with prayer, unconditional love, or biblical morality typically don't talk about their painful upbringing or their current parenting struggles. Pioneer parents read countless books and observe other seemingly perfect parents, but they don't see their own lives and experiences reflected there. So they tend to lock themselves behind walls of silent fear. *Surely,* they reason, *no one else struggles with parenthood the way I do. Surely, no one else raises her voice or cries at night or laments that her parents are a negative influence on her children.*

4. We stand on the shoulders of others. Scientists don't do all their work in isolation. They need the knowledge and experimentation of other researchers who went before them. As early as 1886, scientists had unveiled a possible link between ulcers and bacteria in the stomach lining. Warren and Marshall capitalized on these experiments, furthering their research.

Similarly, pioneer parents must stand on the shoulders of those who have gone before, those who have walked this journey ahead of us. God is gracious to give us mentors in the form of friends, books, and older couples. We cannot parent our children in isolation. We need the grace and knowledge of those around us and those who have gone before us.

5. We count the cost. Since the medical community was not convinced of Warren and Marshall's findings—even though they found the H. pylori bacteria in a majority of their patients who had peptic ulcers—Marshall decided to do something radical. He infected himself by swallowing a large dose of H. pylori. Within a week he began experiencing ulcer symptoms. But once he used antibiotics, his ulcer went away. Still, it took years for this new research to gain wide acceptance.[1]

Marshall was so convinced of the validity of his theory that he took a huge personal risk to prove its accuracy. Likewise, pioneer parents must count the cost of being innovators. Jesus approached several fishermen in ancient Palestine and told them to drop their nets and follow him. They abandoned a way of life that was familiar to them so they could follow Jesus. He says the same thing to us today. He calls us to enter unfamiliar territory, to lay down our agendas, to risk being hurt, to follow him down paths our parents think imbecilic. We must take a personal risk by swallowing the kingdom truth that to live we must die (see Philippians 1:21). Our parents will be slow to come around. And it's entirely possible that they may *never* understand our lifestyle, our Savior, or our way of parenting.

6. We are luminaries. Eventually Warren and Marshall's groundbreaking research was heralded. In 1994 the National Institutes of Health recommended that people with peptic ulcers first go through antibiotic therapy to eliminate H. pylori from their systems. Though misunderstood and maligned, the two doctors eventually gained prominence and stature within the medical community. They became luminaries.

We, too, are luminaries. The word *luminary* comes from the root word for "light." Yet pioneer parents aren't light merely because of our hard labor in obscurity. We are light because the Light of God resides in us. "In him was life, and that life was the light of men. The light shines in the darkness, but the darkness has not understood it" (John 1:4-5). We must bathe our children in Jesus' surprising light, despite the darkness surrounding us.

Like George Bernard Shaw, who acknowledged the prevalence of family skeletons, we all have family-of-origin issues we'd like to conveniently shove back into the closet. We've had sinful parents. We've been sinful parents. Still, God asks us to walk the pioneer-parenting adventure with him, to make the skeletons dance in the light.

God is the only One who can take the skeletons in our lives and breathe life into them for his glory. He causes the circumstances of our lives to work for his good plan so we can become more like Jesus and point the next generation to him and his ability to transform lives.

The apostle Paul penned this oft-quoted verse: "And we know that in all things God works for the good of those who love him, who have been called according to his purpose" (Romans 8:28). It's a lovely sentiment, suitable for greeting cards and wall plaques. But Paul's thought continues: "For those God foreknew he also predestined to be conformed to the likeness of his Son, that he might be the *first-born among many brothers*" (verse 29). God's purpose is for us to be conformed to the likeness of Jesus Christ, who wants to see as many people as possible join his family. God makes the skeletons of our past breathe so we can point the next generation to his life.

God truly is our Pioneer Parent, who dances the path before, behind, and beside us.

Introduction

God Is Bigger Than Our Past

For the LORD will ransom Jacob and redeem them
from the hand of those stronger than they.
—JEREMIAH 31:11

The LORD says, "The people of Israel who survived death
at the hands of the enemy will find favor in the wilderness
as they journey to find rest for themselves."
—JEREMIAH 31:2, *The Net Bible*

The first e-mail I received from my former stepfather ended with these words: "Every saint has a past; every sinner a future." It was a winsome reminder that the God of the universe hears my prayers and longs to save my family members.

I did not learn about God when I was growing up, nor were his principles heralded in my home. My mother married my biological father before I was born, but they divorced soon after. They used to attend church together, but after the divorce, we didn't continue the habit. Oddly, I never called my dad *father;* I called him by his first name.

My mother and I lived with my grandparents while she earned her teaching degree, a time I remember as happy and stable. I recall being reprimanded for riding my tricycle around the corner from Nana's line of sight. I remember the intercom next to my crib where Nana's voice would magically encourage me to go to sleep.

My mother later remarried. Her new husband was an angry mechanic she met in a Laundromat after I turned five. The only detail I remembered about the wedding was that it was held in our backyard, with guests sitting on Indian blankets. Most wore the uniform of the day: tie-dyed shirts, ripped jeans, and long hair.

This was during the early seventies when free love and happy drugs ruled. Protesters shouted angry words about a horrifying war in Vietnam and blocked the interstate highway. My mother and her second husband were caught up in this world—a world I unwittingly joined. They had parties where glazed-eyed hippies sat in circles passing a communal joint; sometimes they were so stoned, they'd pass the sweet-smelling, hand-rolled stick to me. Even then, God had seared a conscience into me—a gift I still thank him for. "No thanks," I'd say and retreat to my bedroom where dolls and stuffed animals greeted me.

My toys were my friends. I had a particular affinity for stuffed animals that no one else wanted. Once, at my baby-sitter's house, I spied a raggedy stuffed cat whose button eyes were gone, leaving circles of unfaded fur as reminders. The cat was forlorn and sad, shoved in a corner. "May I have this, please?" I asked my baby-sitter.

Hoping that perhaps I'd stop pestering her, she nodded yes. I held the kitty to my heart, sang it songs, and cleaned it as best I could. Sometimes I borrowed my dolls' dresses and clothed the stuffed kitty. Somewhere in my five-year-old heart, I suffered when I saw suffering. I had an inner urge to nurture, perhaps because my mother at that point in her life found it difficult to nurture me. Even then, I longed to become a mother someday.

My stuffed animals and dolls provided hours of entertainment, but they couldn't salve my loneliness. One day I asked my mother to play with me. She said, "No. Go out and find a friend." So, as I often did when riding my tricycle at Nana's house, I ventured up the block and around the corner. I saw a young girl playing in a glassed-in porch and walked up to the door and knocked. The girl's mother answered and invited me in. Later my mother found me chattering with my newfound friend, Kimi, who soon became my best friend.

That foundational year of my life was a year I've had to revisit hundreds of times while holding tightly onto God's hand. When each of my children, particularly Sophie and Julia, blew out five candles on their birthday cakes, I panicked. Somehow, seeing their small frames, their bubbling childlikeness, and their innocence transported me back to the year my small frame was violated, my child-likeness darkened.

My first stepfather, the angry mechanic, took apart greasy engines in our living room and yelled at me when I bothered him. That was also the year young thieves stole my tricycle. When I found it later, with the handlebars twisted upside down, one boy said, "It ain't your trike. The handlebars are different. See?" The same boys stole my silver dollars when I sold lemonade on the sidewalk. They handed me a joint rolled with dried oregano leaves to give to my mother as a joke.

But none of that compared to the private hell I experienced nearly every day of my kindergarten year. I attended morning kindergarten. Usually people remember their kindergarten teacher's name, but I don't remember my teacher's name. I can't even tell you what she looked like. I *can* tell you I walked to the baby-sitter's house every day after school, and older boys would come by and ask if I could play. I don't remember their names, but I do remember that they had a stay-at-home mom and a father who was a Boy Scout leader. Every day these brothers, probably in the sixth and eighth grades, took me somewhere—usually ravines in a wooded park—and molested me. One of them once asked me, "Don't you want to have babies someday?" Through stinging tears, I nodded. It had been a dream of mine to become a mommy—just a natural progression from my stuffed-animal nurturing. "Well, then," he said, "this is what you have to do."

The boys used vulgar language to describe their actions. I knew that what they were doing was wrong and that the word they used to describe their assaults was a dirty word. I was afraid to tell my baby-sitter what was going on, mainly because I was afraid I'd get my mouth washed out with soap for swearing. But finally, after too many visits to the forest, I told her in a whisper what they had been doing to me, bad words and all. She bent close, coffee breath polluting my nose, and wheezed, "Well, I'll tell your mother. Don't worry."

Still, the brothers kept coming. Every day. Sometimes they'd get so bold that they'd take me to their home, into their bedroom, and have their way with me while their mom made chocolate-chip cookies for their Scout meetings. I knew I had to take charge, so every day after morning kindergarten I would feign sleep. I'd eat a hasty lunch and lie down on the baby-sitter's bed, squeezing my eyes shut when I heard the inevitable knock at the back door. "She's still napping. I'll send her out when she wakes up," I'd hear the baby-sitter say. The last part of my kindergarten year, I napped a good four hours a day.

It wasn't until much later, in the foothills of adolescence, that I learned the baby-sitter had never told my mother I was being molested. For years I thought my mom had full knowledge of the abuse and just allowed it to continue. With that misconception, I grew up feeling unprotected, unwanted, and unvalued.

My mother and my first stepfather divorced after I finished kindergarten. My mom then married a gentler man. Still, I battled fear—especially during parties in our home. As an only child, I had no one to commiserate with, other than my animals, an imaginary friend named DeeDee, a few dolls, and an occasional friend. At the beginning of the school year, when I walked home as a first grader, I ran into the house, locked the door, and called Nana—a ritual I performed until the sixth grade. Thankfully, that year my mom and stepdad eventually paid for me to go to day care after school, so I wouldn't have to be alone.

Our home was vandalized that same year. When we arrived home I could smell something unusual, even before my stepfather turned the house key. "It smells like a swimming pool," I said.

Inside, the furniture was topsy-turvy. Ketchup streaks lined the walls where framed photos had been ripped down, and the swimming pool smell came from bleach that had been poured down our heat registers. That night the smell of ketchup-bleach made my stomach churn, and I remember feeling alone and frightened. No matter how many blankets I piled on my bed, I shook most of the night.

Every other Sunday I would visit my biological father, who showed an interest in me and exposed me to art galleries, thrift stores, mountain trails, and a slew of artsy friends. He moved in and out of a string of relationships with young women. Once when I asked, horrified, about a bloodstain on his bed, he told me about sex. He seemed very comfortable with the promiscuous side of his life—a part of him that still perplexes me.

My father loved me, or at least he made me the center of his attention when I was around. He threw unusual birthday parties for me with oddly shaped cakes. He also encouraged me to draw and write. Perhaps he wanted to see if I would someday emulate him—he was an incredible black-and-white photographer and a writer.

After finishing his doctoral dissertation in English literature, he decided not to turn it in. Instead, he became a city bus driver, and I sometimes rode along with him on his route. Eccentricity defined my dad, and he assumed the persona of a creative madman, a tragic foreshadowing.

He married a young woman he met on his bus route, and a month before she was to give birth to their first child—my half sister—he died. I was ten years old. I recall sitting in class that day when an announcement came over the school intercom: "Will Mary please come to the office right away?" Alarm tinged the secretary's voice. As I walked down the outside hallway, I noticed the cement-block pattern of the school's walls. Halfway to the office, I knew my father was dead.

In front of the school, my mother and I sat in our green hatchback. She said, "Your father is dead."

Although I knew it was my biological father, I asked, "Which one?"

The following weeks and months blurred together. The man who loved me was dead. The man who took rolls and rolls of black-and-white photos of me would no longer snap another shot. A ten-year-old's grief blanketed me. At night I'd cry. At school I had the meanest teacher of my elementary-school years. When I broke down, she told me, "I used to feel sorry for you, but it's been a month now. You should be over it."

I learned that to be acceptable to others, I had to hide my emotions. Again, I had to take charge of myself and create a facade of well-being. I essentially spent my entire childhood taking care of myself, trying to parent myself.

During junior high I felt, as most pimply, underweight girls do, as if I were trapped, living through an endless loop of *Sixteen Candles*. Awkward and gangly, I tried to fit in with the cool crowd. Mainly, though, I fell apart and ran to the counselor's office several times a week. My mother's third marriage was disintegrating, something that ripped at parts of my heart I couldn't quite identify. The school counselor was a Christian. He listened to me and let me cry. He even gave me a get-out-of-class-free card—a special pass that allowed me to leave whenever I couldn't keep the tears from spilling.

After my eighth-grade year, our extended family gathered at Nana's for Father's Day. I knew it would be the last time I would celebrate that day with my stepfather, because my parents' divorce would soon be final. In the middle of my grandparents' suburban living room, I cracked. Every emotion I had carefully bottled for the sake of my mother, who had a difficult time dealing with my emotions, poured out. My mother asked, "Why are *you* crying?"

Two years later I was weeping again—this time under an evergreen tree at a camp run by Young Life, a ministry for high-school students. A friend in ninth grade had invited me to attend the camp. I was fifteen, and inside I had a raging anger toward my mother, whom I blamed for divorcing my second stepfather. I hated her for driving him away, and I vowed that I would punish her by not meeting her new boyfriend.

But at camp, every time the leader spoke about Jesus, some of my hatred would melt away. My heart hammered in my chest as I heard of the Man who took time for rejected ones, who fed ordinary folks on grassy hills, who touched lepers, who riled the anger of self-righteous pontificators. Every part of me longed for Jesus in a way that only an orphan who longs for parents can.

I had prayed to God all my life. Even when my own father died, I prayed to God. But I didn't know anything about Jesus other than the Christmas story: A baby had been born in a manger in a city called Bethlehem.

Sometimes I saw Jesus as an adult hanging from a cross, but I had no idea why he was there. At Young Life Camp, the speaker told the biblical story of Jesus, simple and graphic, from manger to cross to resurrection. Finally I understood who Jesus was and what he had done for me. Unlike the adults in my life, Jesus had sacrificed himself for me. He laid down everything for me. He took on my hatred, my wayward thoughts, and my dark intentions and died for my sins so I could be set free from them.

That night, after the gospel permeated every cell in my skinny adolescent body, I choked out a prayer to Jesus. I rested against a knobby tree and marveled at the starry sky that peeked through the evergreen canopy. Up there in the heavens sat an eternal Father who would never leave me. That melancholy ache most girls feel when they've lost a father (or, in my case, three fathers) went from hot sadness to cool resignation. I now had a Father who loved me.

Eight years later—after finishing high school and college—I walked down a church aisle wearing white. My mother's boyfriend, the man I had vowed to hate, walked me down the aisle, where I met my mother and my grandfather, who gave me away. Waiting for me was Patrick, my fiancé. In the middle of a storm the northwestern meteorologists called "the Arctic express," we said our vows to love, honor, and cherish each other until death separated us.

The moment the ring circled my finger, I wanted to start having children. Within a year I was pregnant and battling horrific nausea. Three weeks later, just days before Thanksgiving, I was in the hospital having surgery for an ectopic pregnancy. I'd never really yelled at God before. He was my Father, after all, and I knew he was not someone to yell at. But still, in the car on the way to the hospital, I screamed at him. I had believed for a long time that since my life had been difficult growing up, God owed me a perfect life now that I was an adult. I had already experienced enough pain and heartache. I could not trudge through any more.

God let me vent. Lightning didn't strike me dead for shaking my fist at God. A calm sadness filled me as I realized I needed to give God my fierce desire to become a mommy. I had to walk whatever road he laid before me, even if it meant never realizing my dream of having children. The little girl who had sheltered damaged stuffed animals wanted a baby to cuddle. I'd wanted motherhood for as long as I could remember, since episodes of *The Brady Bunch* flickered on our black-and-white TV. Maybe I wanted to create what I never had. Maybe I just needed to give love to someone who was helpless. Maybe I didn't feel my marriage was complete without children. Whatever the reason, I had to give it all to God.

And then Sophie, our eldest, became our own baby in a manger two years after Patrick and I said our vows. A Christmas Eve baby, Sophie was presented to us in a red stocking and a tiny Santa hat. When we took her home, we both stared at the ceiling of our bedroom in what can only be described as utter terror. *What were we thinking? We don't even know how to change diapers, let alone feed, bathe, and protect a baby. What if she breaks?*

PIONEERING PARENTS

From Sophie's first cry until today, when tears wet her cheeks from preteen disappointment, Patrick and I have been on a harrowing journey called *pioneer parenting*. In many ways all of us are pioneer parents, no matter what our upbringing was like. We all have to unlearn things. We all are clueless when it comes to babies, whose instruction manuals are nonexistent and whose noises are coded in cries and burps and giggles.

The question that worried me most when Sophie happily invaded our lives was, *Will she know I love her, or will her childhood reflect mine?* Before our daughter was born, Patrick and I had scoured parenting books. But about one minute into parenthood, we both panicked when we realized that no set of tenets and techniques would help us. As we stared at the ceiling that night, we both realized we needed God's help.

Since I hadn't observed healthy parenting when I was growing up, I turned to books and mentors for advice. I observed other parents and took mental notes of everything they did. I tried to emulate those whose parenting style I admired. I highlighted passages in parenting books and copied bits and pieces into my journal. Still, I felt lost. Because Patrick had grown up in a stable home, I often asked him what his parents did.

The road has not been easy, nor has it been devoid of potholes. Tangled in the whole mess has been God's desire for me to be healed from the emotional trauma of my past—a journey I am still walking today. He's asked me to do the unthinkable: to forgive those who wronged me—another lesson I learn daily. He's asked me to walk a path of humility, seeking forgiveness from my children whenever I yell or rant or demean. Parenthood has become the journey God has used to refine me, to take me beyond my limited strength, to bring me to him.

In this respect, it's been a wonderful adventure. The difficulties pioneer parents face, if viewed redemptively, can be God's means of sanctifying us. Because I am well aware of my frailty, I have the joyful opportunity to reach for his hand, a hand that is stronger and more capable than mine. I've come to relish and appreciate the empowerment of 2 Corinthians 12:9-10, my life verse:

[God] has said to me, "My grace is sufficient for you, for power is perfected in weakness." Most gladly, therefore, I will rather boast about my weaknesses, so that the power of Christ may dwell in me.

Therefore I am well content with weaknesses, with insults, with distresses, with persecutions, with difficulties, for Christ's sake; for when I am weak, then I am strong. (NASB)

Some people never understand the gift of knowing their own lack. Because I am weak, especially in terms of parenting, I have the opportunity to understand God's strength. My weakness, then, becomes a stage for God to reveal his capabilities through me.

It is *because* of my upbringing that I can thank God. Only recently have I been able to truly thank God for the trials of my childhood. He used them to bring me to himself. Had I not had a father-shaped vacuum in my heart, I doubt I would have reached for God underneath that evergreen tree at Young Life Camp. Had I not felt emotionally abandoned, I would not have needed his comfort.

I echo the sentiment Paul expressed to the Christians in ancient Corinth:

> Consider your calling, brethren, that there were not many wise according to the flesh, not many mighty, not many noble; but God has chosen the foolish things of the world to shame the wise, and God has chosen the weak things of the world to shame the things which are strong, and the base things of the world and the despised God has chosen, the things that are not, so that He may nullify the things that are, so that no man may boast before God. (1 Corinthians 1:26-29, NASB)

I was foolish, weak, and impoverished in soul. And yet God chose me. I imagine him looking down from heaven and saying, "See that one there? The girl with the snarled hair and the empty eyes? I am choosing her. I'm going to change her life in such a way that only I can get the glory." In essence, God "Eliza-Doolittled" me. He plucked me from my desperate circumstances in order to change me for his glory. He chose to give me a husband whose love for me resembles his love. And he gave me children to teach me about his nurturing.

Maybe you're in the same place. Maybe you feel foolish and weak. Maybe the thought of trying to parent your children immobilizes you. As a first-generation Christian, you may struggle to even know where to begin. If so, you're in a great place. The premise of this book is not "how to do a bunch of stuff to become a perfect parent"; it's "run to the Father and ask for his help in your weakness."

Perhaps you sing David's song:

> I waited patiently for the LORD;
>
> And He inclined to me and heard my cry.
>
> He brought me up out of the pit of destruction, out of the miry clay,
>
> And He set my feet upon a rock making my footsteps firm.
>
> He put a new song in my mouth, a song of praise to our God;
>
> Many will see and fear
>
> And will trust in the LORD. (Psalm 40:1-3, NASB)

Your past is your pit of destruction. It holds your heart in miry clay. But you no longer need to endure its grip on you. The key is to wait for the Lord to incline himself to you. By now you know you can't pull yourself up by your proverbial bootstraps—that's God's job. He takes your past, your fears, and your demons. He sets your muddy feet on a rock and walks with you on firm ground. Defeat will no longer be your melancholy song. Instead, you will sing praises as he teaches you to parent, as he parents your children through you in your weakness. That way, God will get the glory. And the end result is that "many will see and fear and will trust in the LORD."

EVERY SINNER HAS A FUTURE

The e-mail read, "Every saint has a past; every sinner a future." I received it just this week from my stepfather, the man who helped raise me from age six to fourteen. I hadn't heard from him in decades. Then he contacted me on the eve of my writing of this book to let me know that he had committed his life to Jesus and was passionate about serving him. This man had allowed God to pluck him out of his own pit of destruction, out of his own miry clay.

For those of you who lament the kind of parents you had, for those who worry that God's arm isn't long enough to reach your extended family, take heart. Keep praying. Someday you might receive an e-mail or phone call proving just how long God's arm is. He longs to lift people from deep pits. He did that for me. He also did it for my stepfather.

He'll do the same for you and for those you love. Ask him, and reach up for his strong arm.

Part I

Healing for the Past

The first step of the pioneer-parenting journey is asking God to heal us. We bring everything into our parenting, every pain, every injury, and every bitterness. As pioneer parents, we owe it to our children to run to God first, weeping at his feet, asking him to fill us where we're empty and bolster us where we're weak. *Only* through his healing can we hope to love and nurture the next generation.

It is through the avenue of our pain that God does new things in our lives. He creates beauty from the ashes of our past. He takes our pain and constructs a monument to his grace.

Perhaps you picked up this book because you've walked the avenue of pain. In this section I hope the Lord will expose your heart, laying it bare before his tender gaze. If you let him, he will heal it—for the sake of his glory and your children's joy.

"I'm Afraid of the Sky Ghost!"

Realizing the Truth About Safe Places

> *The name of the LORD is a strong tower;*
> *the righteous run to it and are safe.*
> —PROVERBS 18:10

Unsafe again. A chill tickled my six-year-old spine as I spied the sky ghost. He illuminated the rectangle of darkened sky I viewed through the picture window of our small home. Circling, the ghost seemed to be watching me. As he searched the horizon, I felt sure he would light on me. Maybe he would kill me.

Alone in the living room, I had nobody to shelter me from the sky ghost, other than two cats and a stuffed kangaroo. The hardwood floor chilled my skinny feet as I worried behind the drapes. I peeked at the sky through parted fingers, wishing my mom and stepdad would come into the room and protect me from the ghost's swooping tentacles.

But they didn't.

Frozen, I watched for the Datsun sedan to pull up outside, come to a squeaky halt, and deliver someone who could comfort me. I fantasized about Tarzan parents who would swing in and rescue me at just the right moment. Problem was, my parents weren't in the business of rescuing me from my fears or offering sky-ghost explanations.

The sky ghost circled back around, looking for me. As I crouched lower behind the curtains and closed my fingers around my eyes, I remembered the ghost stories my parents' marijuana-smoking buddies told during hazy parties. Although I'm sure they weren't telling the stories to scare me, they spun chilling yarns about the haunted house I lived in.

"There's a ghost in your attic." A man whose face I can't recall exhaled sweet-smelling smoke and pulled me closer. "If you listen real good, you can hear her chair creak as it rocks back and forth—right above your bedroom light fixture—usually around midnight. You have to listen close, though."

I swallowed hard and nodded.

During another party someone else warned me about the cabinet ghost, a specter whose secret delight was opening and shutting kitchen cabinets while I slept. "When you wake up, do you ever notice open cabinets?"

I nodded.

"There's the proof right there."

Another time someone flung back our fraying oriental rug, revealing a brownish stain on the hardwood floor the size of a large dog. "See?" he said. "Someone was murdered here. This is a blood stain."

Standing on that same floor, I ducked away from the sky ghost. Then I ran past the kitchen's opened cabinets for the comfort of my room. Instead of finding refuge, I looked at the light fixture, sure the attic ghost would rattle it above my head. I dove into bed and prayed that the sky ghost wouldn't find me under my covers.

That night something as benign as a searchlight announcing Big Bob's Car-O-Rama Blowout Sale became a haunting reminder that the world was a scary place, and that I, a spooked six-year-old, had to face it alone.

The story has been told of a young boy whose mother tucked him into bed at the onset of a storm and left the room to attend to her evening chores. When the crash of thunder shook the house and lightning flashed across the sky, the worried mother returned to her son's room to make sure he was okay. She found him standing in front of the window with a big grin on his face as the lightning flickered on his face.

"Son," his mother asked, "why are you smiling? Aren't you scared?"

"No, Mom! Isn't it great? God just took my picture!"

That's the difference between growing up in a safe home and an unsafe one:

The child who feels safe approaches a storm, smiling for God's camera, while the child who doesn't feel safe cowers alone, hiding from sky ghosts.

Most parents want to create an environment where their children feel safe. Yet you may have grown up in a place where fear reigned. Or perhaps it was rage. Or violence. Or an obsession with body fat. We all come from dysfunctional families, because all families are made up of sinners. But there are degrees of dysfunction, and chances are you or someone you love grew up in a threatening environment. You may be haunted by the fear that you will parent your children the way you were parented.

My sincere prayer is that the principles in this book, along with the power of the Holy Spirit, will help you establish a safe place for your children to smile for God's camera.

THE ONE SAFE PLACE

To pioneer a safe, loving place for our children, we need to realize that outside of our relationship with Jesus Christ, there is no safe place. This world is racked with terrorism, child abductions, drug abuse, suicide, and a host of other malevolent forces. Jesus said, "In the world you have tribulation, but take courage; I have overcome the world" (John 16:33, NASB). If you grew up in a home that didn't emulate Christian ideals or love, chances are you did not grow up in a safe place.

My friend Jack remembers being four years old when his mother gripped his small shoulders and shook him violently while screaming, "Do you hear me?" When he was older and not as easy to shake, she'd pin him against the wall and slap both sides of his face.

Jack also remembers his feelings of helplessness on a rare visit to his father. "I was twelve then. Everyone, including my dad, was smoking pot. All I could do was ride my bike to the lake and cry—alone. It got to be that withdrawing or running away became my response. If I ever approached my mom about anything troubling, she responded with such hostility that I learned not to approach her at all. I stayed by myself." Jack came to understand that if he was going to be safe, he'd have to take care of himself.

Jack's example is extreme, but even the families whose Olan Mills portraits exude normalcy are flawed. We all share Adam and Eve's lineage of sin. Hopefully, we've realized by now that the only safe place isn't a location but a Person: Jesus. The psalmist acknowledged that the only true refuge from our earthly fears is found in God's strong arms: "I will lie down and sleep in peace, for you alone, O LORD, make me dwell in safety" (Psalm 4:8).

My own longing for Jesus, a Companion who would never leave me, fueled a lifelong quest. Growing up, I heard God's name spoken in profanity. Yet I still hunted for him in that unsafe place called home. I prayed to him when I was afraid. But even so, I was not safe.

Not having a safe place grew a weed of insecurity in my heart, and the tendrils still wrap around my heart today. Growing up in an unprotected environment, I seldom felt taken care of. But when older boys ripped away my five-year-old innocence, I realized that I alone had to take care of myself. When burglars vandalized our house, in my fear I did not feel safe.

The result of this neglect was twofold. It gave me a passionate desire to love my own children fiercely, but it also made me worry that I would repeat my parents' mistakes. Would my children feel as unsafe as I did when I was a girl? That worry still haunts me today.

Although it is naive to think we can provide an entirely safe place for our children, it *is* possible with God's help to foster a warm, secure parental bond with a child. Not only is it possible, but it's essential. Our children's first task is attaching to a person who will (hopefully) protect them.

Many pioneer parents didn't form such an attachment with their own parents, so they are unfamiliar with the safety that comes from a parent's love. We may instinctively know what a safe place does *not* look like, but because of our negative experiences, it is difficult to picture what a safe place *does* look like. We need to understand the meaning and characteristics of safe places—both for our own benefit and for the health of our children. With that in mind, consider the following characteristics:

1. A safe place is a refuge. Just as a wildlife refuge protects animals from bullets and arrows, a safe home protects a child from life's barbs. It's a place where a child can fall apart and not fear judgment. Last year our daughter Sophie was coming undone the moment she stepped off the school bus. For a while I worried about this, questioning what was happening at school to churn up so many emotions. Besides concluding that fifth-grade hormonal changes had a role in this, I realized that my daughter was falling apart because she could. We have succeeded, at least on some level, in creating a safe environment where she's free to express her emotions.

When I was a junior-high teacher, I noticed an interesting dynamic in two types of students. When I met the parents of some students who were out of control at school, the parents were often surprised to hear about their child's outbursts. They'd say something like, "Well, she isn't that way at home," and then they'd look at me as if I were Mephistopheles in the flesh for suggesting such a thing.

Sometimes, when I met with the parents of an I'll-do-anything-for-an-A student, they'd raise their eyebrows and say, "He certainly doesn't act that way at home. He's been climbing the walls." The kids who worked diligently at school, who did extra credit to get an A-plus, seemed to have the freedom to fall apart at home, to let down after a day of school stress.

My unscientific proposition is this: Safe homes allow children to fall apart; unsafe homes don't. The truth is, we all fall apart, and God designed the family as a holy refuge—a place where both acne *and* anger can erupt. It doesn't mean a family is a place to take license; instead, it's a safe place where love overlooks the acne of character and enables a child to work through anger.

2. A safe place is a demonstration of God's parenting skills. We are representatives of God to our children. Whether we grew up in a stable or a chaotic home, our task is to uncover the true characteristics of God that our parents' sinful natures marred. God is not the same as our earthly parents, even the good ones. As our heavenly Parent, he is not critical, condemning, injurious, aloof, or neglectful. Even the best parents fall short of demonstrating God's perfect, unconditional love. And so will we.

But we can grow in godliness as we raise our children. Part of successful pioneer parenting is unlearning old patterns, pressing into God's warm embrace and parental heart, and learning his ways. Why look back? Why try to understand our family of origin? Isn't the old swept away with the dawning of our new lives in Christ? It's true that, because Christ died for our sins, we have the surprising pleasure of having been justified in God's sight, which means we are utterly accepted by a holy God. Our histories, though, aren't magically removed when we become Christians. In the book *Unclaimed Baggage,* authors Don and Jan Frank expand on this idea. "Forgetting the past in that sense is no mark of spirituality. God neither ignores nor plays down our ruins. If God doesn't ignore, deny, play down, or annihilate our histories, what does he do with them? *He redeems them.*"[1]

God is in the redeeming business. He takes our broken pasts, infuses them with his healing, and through the Holy Spirit enables us to forge new parenting paths. The apostle Paul encouraged the Christians living in ancient Ephesus with these words: "God can do anything, you know—far more than you could ever imagine or guess or request in your wildest dreams! He does it not by pushing us around but by working within us, his Spirit deeply and gently within us" (Ephesians 3:20, MSG).

We have the privilege as pioneer parents of demonstrating God's nature to our children, but we cannot do that unless God redeems our broken pasts and parents our kids through us.

3. A safe place is grace infused. Because the one truly safe place is in the arms of our heavenly Father, if we as parents are to provide a safe place for our children, we need to demonstrate grace. Jesus modeled this concept when he welcomed the children who clambered onto his grace-filled lap:

> Then little children were brought to Jesus for him to place his hands on them and pray for them. But the disciples rebuked those who brought them.
>
> Jesus said, "Let the little children come to me, and do not hinder them, for the kingdom of heaven belongs to such as these." (Matthew 19:13-14)

My friend Jack, now a parent, wants to create a home of grace. "I want my daughters to know there is nothing they can do to make me *not* love them."

His daughter once asked, "Daddy, will you love me if I hit my sister?"

Jack responded, "Honey, I would be very disappointed if you hit your sister, and I would have to discipline you, but I will *always* love you."

That's a grace-infused home.

4. A safe place is a place where a child doesn't wonder about love. A child does not live in a safe place if he or she is constantly wondering, *Do my parents really love me? If I died, would Mommy miss me?* To feel safe, children must know from the top of their tangle-haired heads to the bottom of their toe-jammed toes that their parents love them—no matter what.

I was a pest as a child. Because I didn't feel that my mother cared about me, I constantly asked, "Do you love me?" I asked for hugs and relished her spontaneous affection. As pioneer parents, it's imperative that we watch for cues from our children. When mine pester me to hug them, I know I am failing to instill a deep knowledge that they are loved. I want my children to wonder wide-eyed at the God who gave them life. I don't want them to wonder whether I love them.

5. *A safe place has clear boundaries and expectations.* A certain school had an unfenced playground. Children, afraid of the nearby street traffic, huddled near the playground equipment during recess and avoided the open field near the street. A smart principal erected a fence around the field, and suddenly the children ran and played freely—right up to the edge of the street. A simple chain-link fence provided a boundary that created freedom and spontaneity inside its protective enclosure.

Parents, because they love their children, will set boundaries by letting them know what is and isn't allowed. If there are no family rules, chaos results—not necessarily overtly, but in the heart of a child. Children who have to determine their own set of rules never really know where they stand with their parents, and they are ill equipped to determine rules in the first place. A child without boundaries growing up will struggle in adulthood to learn to erect appropriate boundaries.

6. *A safe place gives children freedom to fail.* A safe place, however, isn't a straitjacket of rules and regulations. Pioneer parents need not become Pharisaical legalists, doling out so many parameters that they confuse and overwhelm their children. In a safe place, realistic ground rules are set. Children who break those simple rules are disciplined with love. Just as Jesus Christ disciplines us for our own good, so we must discipline our children. But we stop short of barraging them with reminders of their failures. Children will fail to meet our expectations; it's one of life's realities. Dusting our children off, tousling their hair, and lovingly setting them back on their feet helps them learn that failure is a normal part of life.

When we freely admit our failures—even our parenting mistakes—to our children, we create a safe place for our families. We demonstrate the truth that at times we all fail, and we all are in desperate need of God's forgiveness, grace, and empowerment.

Our goal should be to correct our children's behavior while still delighting in their individuality. A stable home provides freedom to fail within the context of grace. For our children to grow up into autonomous adults who revel in their God-given individuality, they must understand the nuances of God's unconditional love. We give them that understanding as we live out unconditional love in our own lives.

YOU ARE A GOOD PARENT

The insecurity I've nursed about providing a safe home for my children is at times a nondescript fear; at other times it strangles me. A few moments stand out to me, little glimpses, really, that help me continue down this pioneering path.

One snapshot is when my friend Heidi came to visit in 1999. At the end of her stay, she held my gaze. "You're a good mother, Mary. Your children know you love them."

Her words salved my fearful heart. Growing up, I felt I was in the way. I worried that I would project that same feeling onto my children. Knowing an outsider saw that my children knew I loved them eased much of my worry.

Another snapshot. Just two years after Heidi's visit, I was sitting on the love seat in our Texas living room. In the quiet of evening with the kids tucked in bed, the Lord said, "Mary, I want you to say 'I am a good mother' out loud."

"Really?" I asked, without giving voice to my thoughts.

"Yes."

It took me a long time to say the words. I'm not sure why I was so afraid; perhaps I was worried that I would sound self-absorbed or self-important if I spoke them into the air.

"I am a good mother," I whispered.

As soon as I said it, the noose around my heart loosened; I gasped, breathing in free air for the first time in nine years of parenthood. As I look back on those freedom-filled words, I realize that in saying them aloud, I was declaring God's ability to heal me.

God is in the business of gathering hurting people and transforming them into dependent followers of his Son. It is our weakness that *allows* God to do his work. The apostle Paul emphasized this when he said,

Isn't it obvious that God deliberately chose men and women that the culture overlooks and exploits and abuses, chose these "nobodies" to expose the hollow pretensions of the "somebodies"? That makes it quite clear that none of you can get by with blowing your own horn before God. Everything that we have—right thinking and right living, a clean slate and a fresh start—comes from God by way of Jesus Christ. (1 Corinthians 1:27-30, MSG)

Through God's grace, I hope my children will never have to write a book that begins, "I didn't grow up in a safe home."

2

"I'd Rather Forget the Past"

Enjoying the Freedom of Finally Telling the Truth

Then you will know the truth, and the truth will set you free.
—JOHN 8:32

It has been an excruciating journey to tell the truth about my upbringing, not so much because of the bravery required to tell it but because in doing so, I've had to mourn its aftermath. Truth telling has been part of my quest in becoming a successful pioneer parent. In order to break unhealthy patterns from the past, I have had to recognize them, speak them plainly, mourn them, and then let them go.

Like a mangled package from the post office, with tape and paper ripped and contents spilling out, the truth never comes to us neatly wrapped. It is messy. It takes time to unravel. It is elusive, at times veering this way and that—so much so that we career around it, dizzied. And we are not the only ones who experience the effects as we investigate our past. Our extended families also are affected by the process.

In my desire to understand more about my early years, I wrote letters and called family members. I had an insatiable desire to return to the "scene of the crime" and understand afresh what really happened. Unfortunately (and understandably) my family members didn't welcome my inquisitiveness. "Why go back there?" someone asked me. "I don't think about the past anymore. It's too painful."

Still, I had to understand what went on "back there." As an adult, though, I realize that truth is an elusive commodity, slippery at best. How I saw my childhood then may not reflect the entire truth. My knee-high perspective is not all there is. So when I share stories of my upbringing with you, I am sharing from my childhood point of view, not from anyone else's.

As a parent, I know that my children will see their childhoods much differently than I see them. Similarly, my parents will see things I didn't see. I know that only the Lord sees my story in its entirety, but I have benefited greatly by understanding and sharing how I felt as a child. As I tell my story, it is not my intention to indict my parents; I simply want to share my limited perspective and paint a picture of how God used the pain of my upbringing to bring me to himself. The story is really about him.

RUNNING LAPS AROUND MY CHILDHOOD

When I was in college, working through the story of my upbringing, I did a simple exercise. While running on the indoor track, I realized that twenty laps made one mile—and I was twenty years old. So with each lap, I recounted what happened to me during each year of my life and asked God to help me sort out each experience. It went something like this:

Lap 1: As I ran, I prayed, "Lord, I know my conception was an accident, but thank you that you created me and willed me to be born. I wish so much that my mom and dad had stayed together. Their marriage was so brief—full of things I don't yet understand. Help me have a long-lasting marriage someday, Lord. Help me learn from my past."

Lap 4: "Lord, thank you for sending me to my grandparents, for the stability their home gave me. Thank you that although I felt the strong hand of discipline from a worried grandmother, I knew her love. Help me understand discipline, Lord. Help me remember the importance of stability when I have children of my own."

Lap 5: "This was an awful year. The rapes still haunt my dreams at night. I forgive those faceless boys. But help me get beyond the fear that roils my insides every time I get close to a man. Thank you that you seared me with a red-hot conscience, even at five, that when the joints were passed and offered to me, I refused, knowing that smoking pot was wrong. Thank you for taking my second father out of my life. He was an angry, disinterested man. Help me forgive my mother for her lifestyle that year."

Lap 10: "I still don't know why you took my earthly father. I miss him. Yet I am perplexed by some of his behaviors toward me and toward young women. Help me sort this all out. Help me forgive him. Help me forgive my mother for telling me I should get over his loss quickly. Thank you for giving me a friend. You must've known I needed her. Even though I didn't yet know you, I sensed your presence when I prayed."

Lap 13: "I think my anger scalded me this year. A deep rage filled my heart, and I had nowhere to place it. Thank you for giving me a Christian school counselor who understood my anger. Help me afresh to forgive my mother for the breakup of her third marriage. Enable me to mourn my stepfather's absence after the divorce. He'd promised he would always be in my life, but he left me behind. Thank you for giving me friends, even as I felt like taking myself from this world. Forgive me for contemplating that."

Lap 15: "Lord, I found you that year. Right under that blessed hemlock tree. Thank you for drawing me gently to yourself. I remember my heart pounding in my rib cage every time I heard the name Jesus. The last fifteen minutes of Young Life Club meetings was a time I longed for each week, when the leader would tell of the God-Man who commanded the seas and winds and loved me enough to die for me. Thanks for Young Life Camp. Thanks for pointing your amazing hand from heaven right on top of my bowed head. Lord, my mom didn't like it when I came home and told her about my newfound relationship with you. She told me I was in a cult and said that when she died, that was it. No heaven. No hell. She's been against my relationship with you ever since. Help me to love her, forgive her, and live a life worthy of you."

I kept running and praying until, breathless and sore legged, I finished the mile. I prayed that someday God would surprise me with a husband and children and allow me, through his grace, to avoid some of my parents' mistakes. I thanked God for the buckets of tears I cried, remembering that he recorded every one: "Record my lament; list my tears on your scroll—are they not in your record?" (Psalm 56:8). I mourned what might have been—a secure childhood that I never knew. I asked God to show me my sin. I counted the times he stretched out his long arm to rescue me and draw me to himself. I thanked him that my mother had changed, that her lifestyle was decidedly different, her choices wiser.

Even today, I count my years and pray through each one—now, more to count my blessings than to remember the pain. It serves as a good reminder that life is hard, but God is my hand holder, even as I gasp for air on lap thirty-eight.

RIGOROUS HONESTY

I read a phrase once that captures what's important in remembering the past: rigorous honesty. Like running laps on a track, honesty is laborious. If you want to rear your children in a new way, invigorated by the gentle whispers of the Holy Spirit, you must first revisit the dark places and let God's Spirit shine his light into the dusty corners. If you don't let the Lord walk with you through your difficult past, you will not experience the joy of rearing your own children in a healthy environment. Counselors and authors Don and Jan Frank assert, "We tend to replicate what we have known with little thought or intention, simply because we are doing what comes naturally or is familiar."[1]

It's understandable that we would prefer to forget our difficult upbringings. We want to carefully sweep away the agony, the wishing for a Brady Bunch family, the feeling of deep insecurity that wrapped its tentacles around us. We don't want a soul to see us as we were then—vulnerable and wanting. So we become stuffers, shoving uncomfortable secrets behind closet doors under the stairs of our conscious minds. We hide the door keys in our pockets, but when we come to Jesus, we say, "Clean my house, Lord. Clean me up inside." We sing all sorts of important songs about his making things new and polishing us clean.

And we somehow justify keeping our past locked in our closets. "Hey, the Bible says that God makes all things new. The past is gone.[2] I'm new. The closet, well, it needs to stay locked, thank you very much." But like Frodo grasping onto to the one Ring, we grip the closet key tightly in our sweaty hands. In quiet moments, Jesus asks us to give him the key as an act of worship, to open up every area of our lives to him, but still we hold on. Not even God gets to look in there. It's just too scary.

The rigorous truth is this: If we long to get beyond the pain of our past and move toward forgiveness and wholeness, we must hand Jesus the keys to our closet doors. We must be brave enough to let him walk through the darkness with us. He can bring meaning to our suffering if we dare to let him. He will take one pain at a time and heal it. Then he will take another. He can shed light on the sin in our lives. He can heal the wounds of the past so we won't be as prone to inflict the same wounds on our children.

Most of us, however, are too afraid. Most of us would rather skate along the surface of life with an all-is-well facade, while we crumble inside. Most of us would rather believe that when we come to Christ, he magically sweeps away all the pain, gives us new lives, and promises wholeness from the start.

Most of us believe that the truth will set us free, but we'd rather think of truth in abstract terms. We'd rather not delve into sticky issues from the past. *That's not truth,* we reason. *Truth has to do with ethereal things, with beauty and grace and righteousness.*

There's an old saying that goes, "You have to feel in order to heal." Feeling hurts. Telling the truth about our childhoods involves painful reflection, mourning. Healing never comes from hiding.

Proclaiming the Truth

To experience God's healing—especially as we seek to parent our children in a renewed and redeeming way—there are several things we must do. And each of these things has to do with hearing and proclaiming the truth about our childhoods and ourselves.

Proclaim the Truth About Your Childhood

My friend Stacey was asking questions that made me uncomfortable, so I simply told her, "My father loved me." I couldn't meet her eyes as I poked at my scrambled eggs.

She was probing, and her questions were getting more pointed. "How do you know that?" she asked.

"Well, you know, he took me places—museums, the mountains."

"You've said that already."

I chewed another bite of egg. "Well, he did *some* strange things—things that made me feel uncomfortable."

"Like what?" Her eyes were steady, locked on mine.

I suddenly developed an even more intense interest in my breakfast. But then I took a deep breath and answered her question. I stated what my father had done, but I did it in such an antiseptic way that it alarmed me. Saying it aloud but without emotion worried me.

"Mary," she said, this time holding my teary gaze, "that is *not* love."

Right then, haloed in the light of the Maltby Café, I watered my breakfast plate with my tears while my best friend prayed.

After a few gulps of air, I said, "But, Stacey, if I admit that my father didn't understand healthy love, then I have to admit that, essentially, *no one* knew how to love me—that in terms of relationship with both my parents, I was an orphan."

Later, when we talked about that conversation, Stacey said she felt the Lord prompting her to ask those painful questions. I had droned on and on about how I struggled to forgive my mother and how much I longed to sincerely love her, when Stacey stopped me and said, "Sometimes we direct our anger at the other parent, when really it's the unmentioned parent we have issues with." That's when she started asking about my father, peeling away yet another layer of my childhood story.

Like the acrid rings of a potent onion, we discover the stinging pain of our childhood only by peeling away its layers. The hard part is that each new layer peeled away brings more tears. Sometimes God brings spouses or counselors into our lives to help us get honest about the past. Sometimes, as in my case, God uses a close friend to peel away an emotionally painful layer. I don't think I'd be at the place I am now in terms of understanding and accepting my upbringing had it not been for alert and ruthlessly kind friends like Stacey.

Perhaps the most interesting aspect of truth telling is that it doesn't usually happen when you're alone staring at the ceiling. It is within the context of loving, stable relationships that God births truth. All of us long to be loved authentically, even with our warts and prickles and insecurities. We may hide our deep pain for years, but with that secrecy comes an unsettled feeling that if the truth were told, no one would really love us.

A blessed transformation comes, then, when friends and spouses ask pointed questions and wait quietly for our responses. Stacey let the awkward silence hang in the air for several minutes at the café while I wrestled with her question. When

I faced the dark truth that I didn't feel parental love as a child, she was there to share her friendship with me. That's the great paradox of truth. If you tell it to safe people, you may have to mourn a terrible loss, but you gain a deeper friendship that is based on truth. By telling Stacey my painful truth, I gave her the opportunity to shoulder my pain, and I felt a freedom that had eluded me for years. I also experienced Stacey's unconditional acceptance.

Telling the truth to safe and trusted people is a necessary step. It breeds relational intimacy. However, not everyone in your life will love your newfound interest in truth, especially if you spout it off at inopportune moments. I liken the passion for truth telling to the zeal of a new convert. When I first became a Christian, I told the world about Jesus. I told the guy at the gas station, the new exchange student, my unsuspecting family. But as I walked longer with Jesus and learned to sense the prompting of the Holy Spirit, I waited for his guidance before I spoke.

It's the same when we begin to uncover the hard truth about our childhoods. We have to be cautious about what we share and how we share it, and even whether to share it at all. I grew up in an extended family that did not allow conflict. Sure, we gossiped about everyone else behind their backs, but we'd never confront a family member directly. Everything was perfect on the outside—all relationships appeared intact. So for me to come in and stir up the waters has been difficult for my family. I've had to let go of needing to process my pain with my biological family, especially since it often results in their denying the truth. Instead, I've understood afresh that my true family is made up of fellow Christians—the body of Christ. I go to them when I am in pain. I am vulnerable before them.

My biological family is nonconfrontational, but yours might be volatile. Speaking the truth in those families can be injurious and sometimes devastating. Or your family might be dismissive. When my friend Jack began to speak up about his mother's abuse, members of his extended family actually laughed. "When my family talks about the way my mom shook me, they make it a big joke," he says. "No one is willing to really bring it out into the open—at least on a serious level."

The keys to telling the truth are wisdom and understanding. As a teenager, I was an overproclaimer. I'd share my life story with any new friend, right down to the embarrassing details. After my junior year of high school, I went on a week-long hike in the mountains with friends from Young Life and spouted off my story to a college leader. He looked at me, perplexed, and asked, "Are you sure you want to share this with me?"

At first I shrugged his question from my mind. But later I realized his wisdom. It's not wise to share everything with everyone. I had such a deep-seated desire for people to think I was okay that I felt compelled to tell them the details of my upbringing. Secretly I hoped they'd think, *Wow, she's pretty amazing, coming through all that.* The older (and hopefully wiser) I get, the more strategic I become in sharing my story. Now when I share, it's with a view to redemption.

I've had to realize that I will never have a deep relationship with my family of origin, at least not until they acknowledge the truth themselves. Initially I believed that if I forgave everyone, reconciliation would be automatic—just as watering a seed produces a flower. The hitch was that I could water that ground until my fingers wrinkled, but it remained barren—no life erupted. It took me years to understand that forgiveness is unilateral: It involves only my tipping the watering can. "If it is possible, as far as it depends on you," the apostle Paul said, "live at peace with everyone" (Romans 12:18). I forgive those who have wronged me, but that doesn't guarantee that they will respond.

In contrast, reconciliation is bilateral; it always involves two people. I can water the soil, but if no seed of willingness is there, I can't expect a flower to grow, no matter how much I water. Reconciliation is a beautiful, amazing thing, but it can only be apprehended through honesty and repentance. If someone is not willing to be honest and doesn't see the need to repent, then reconciliation is impossible.

Proclaim the Truth About Yourself

In addition to proclaiming the truth about your upbringing, it's important not to neglect confessing your own sin as you examine that upbringing. It's not hard for me to look back now and see how selfish I was, but for many years, I pointed my finger only at my family—at how bad things were. As Jesus said, it's always easier to notice the speck in someone else's eye and overlook the log lodged in our own eyes (see Luke 6:41-42). I had a lot of logs in my eyes. It hasn't been until recently that I've been able to see the part I played in my upbringing.

As an only child, my world revolved around me. I longed for material things and manipulated my mother into buying my affection. I was stubborn, evasive, and a snoop. I lived for myself and my own pleasure, especially when hormones ignited my vocal cords. I would yell and slam doors. I was ungrateful, hoarding, obsessive.

I used to believe that as I got closer to Jesus, I'd sin less. But I've found that the closer I get to him, the dirtier I feel, and the more apt I am to confess my sins—even the sins of my childhood. A true mark of maturity isn't sinlessness; it's confession, brokenness, and rigorous honesty. If you think you're sinless in terms of your past, you've failed to look deeply at yourself.

Besides admitting our sins, we must also get to the place where we can see the positive things our parents did. Now that I've walked through the negative pictures that darkened my view of my childhood, I've been able to recapture happy memories. Once, my parents picked me up from day care on horseback. I had never felt more honored—all the kids pushed their noses through the chain-link fence, wishing they were me. I remember my mom's generosity, how she sacrificed to give me wonderful Christmases and birthday parties, how she surprised me one year with a much-pined-for piano. I love that my mom would not allow me to disrespect her and that she valued my obedience. She provided everything I needed, and often what I wanted: a car, an education, braces. Though she worked full time, she made an effort to go to my concerts when I sang solos. My journal contains notes full of love and concern that she has written to me. Had I not walked through healing, these wonderful memories would have stayed locked away in my head.

I remember my father's love of art and nature and the hours we spent together enjoying both. I remember the books he illustrated and wrote just for me. I remember the boxes of black-and-white snapshots taken just of me, as if I were a great work of art. I think of my father's widow, who talked about Jesus when I was a teenager, plowing the soil so that when I was ready, the seed sown in my heart would take root.

Once we've walked through rigorous honesty about our pain, a new door opens, revealing snapshots of grace in our childhoods. I took a run around my neighborhood today. I didn't recount each year of my life with every lap. Instead, I thanked God for bringing me to where I am today: a pioneer parent who tells the truth and has experienced God's healing.

The truth does, in fact, set us free.

"But You Don't Know How Bad Things Were!"

Accepting God's Healing for Past Family Trauma

*Sweet are the uses of adversity, which like the toad, ugly
and venomous, wears yet a precious jewel on his head.*
—WILLIAM SHAKESPEARE

Stories. We all play a part in them—in our own, in other people's stories that mingle with our own, in stories of people we admire, of people far away, of ancient people. When I hear someone share his or her story, I enjoy recognizing the redemptive hand of God woven through it. When I read about someone's journey, I feel as if I were a part of the journey, learning lessons alongside that person. When I tell my own story, I want to weave God's redemption through it, and I want to invite you to join me in the journey.

I'd like to paraphrase three stories from the life of Jesus. There are parallels with my own journey toward healing—and with your journey as well.

DO YOU WANT TO GET WELL?

I've often puzzled over a question Jesus asked the lame man in John 5. The man, who hadn't walked in thirty-eight years, was lying by a pool in Bethesda. If I could write the script, I'd have Jesus say, "Wow, that's a long time to be lame! How are you doing? I really empathize with your pain."

Instead, Jesus was blunt. "Do you want to get well?" he asked.

"Well...er...uh," the man stammered. He gave a litany of reasons why he had never been healed and lamented the fact that he couldn't manage to crawl fast enough to the pool's edge when the angel stirred the waters. Someone always got there ahead of him.

"Oh, that's hard! Poor man." These are words I would have said if I were Jesus. But not Jesus. He simply said, "Get up! Pick up your mat and walk."

The man obeyed, and as he lifted himself up, legs that hadn't moved in decades were suddenly energized. Atrophied muscles became sinewy, ready to work. Bent knees straightened, and the man walked. He was healed by the Maker of all legs.[1]

HEALING IS A PROCESS

Next is the story about a blind man in chapter 8 of Mark's gospel. Imagine being blind. Unless you are reading this text with your fingers, it's nearly impossible to relate to the complete darkness that envelops a blind person, even when his or her eyes are open. Imagine going through life being both intrigued and frustrated by the sound of ocean waves or the smell of daisies. And then one day, while your vacant eyes stare at blackness, a friend approaches you. "I found a man who heals people with a word or a touch. I want you to meet him."

"But," you protest, "a man like this—if he really does what you're saying (and frankly, I find that hard to believe)—wouldn't want to bother with me. He'd be far too important for that."

"Come on! I'll take you to him," your friend insists.

Something in you resists. For so long you've been accustomed to life as a blind person. For so long you have entertained and then discarded that useless commodity called hope. Still, since your friend insists, you take blind steps toward meeting the healing man.

"There he is," your companion says.

You shrink back. As you do, your companion's hand slips from your grasp. Surrounded by sounds from a village you've never visited before, you shudder. In desperation, you touch your face in order to root yourself to this unfamiliar place.

Then another hand engages yours. Wordless, the Owner of the hand leads you away from the village. Silence.

Did someone just spit?

Whoever grabbed your hand is spitting into your eyes. Wanting to recoil yet irresistibly drawn, you feel the same hands on your face. As you blink, your dark vision lightens.

"Do you see anything?" the Man with the hands asks.

All you really want to do is gaze on the hazy face of the One whose spittle has lightened your vision. Lifting your eyes, you see dim vertical shapes moving around. You recall your encounters with trees—of running into them and becoming aware of their tall, lanky stature. You tell the Man, "I see people; they look like trees walking around."

The Man places his hands on your eyes. At once your eyes are seeing the world in 20/15 vision—in Lasik clarity. With crystal-clear vision, you see the face of the Man who gave you sight. You weep. You laugh. You dance. After so many years of blindness, this one miraculous event has restored your sight. Once you were blind, but now you see. The One who made every eye has healed yours.[2]

WHAT DOES THIS HAVE TO DO WITH YOUR JOURNEY?

For many years I puzzled over the question Jesus asked the man who couldn't walk: "Do you want to get well?" I was so trapped by my own pain that I couldn't understand this question. After I met Jesus at fifteen, I devoured the Bible. I highlighted catchy verses about being made new and the past being put behind me. I gravitated toward the Jesus who healed, and I claimed my own emotional healing. I wouldn't let the old pain back in because I had been healed.

But at the same time, I battled with obsession and fear.

As a fatherless girl, I was obsessed with having a boyfriend. I wrote pages and pages in my journal about my loneliness. I questioned why God wouldn't "let" me have a boyfriend, as if this were a commodity God was denying me. I railed against the wisdom of the Almighty. (In retrospect, I fall on my knees and thank God a thousand times that he didn't answer my "Give me a boyfriend" prayer. Who knows what promiscuity or abuse could have resulted!)

But as soon as a boy expressed interest in me, my fears came into play. I shut down emotionally and withdrew from the interested young man. I justified this with religious language. "He's just not a strong Christian. I am being holy by shunning his advances." I had read enough Elisabeth Elliot books to be determined to remain pure for my marriage bed. Secretly, I hoped I could abstain from kissing until the minister said, "You may kiss the bride."

At night, though, the fears I experienced by day ran crazy races in my mind. I couldn't quiet my thoughts, couldn't silence fear's roaring. A college journal entry reads, "Now I am too afraid to be silent in the night. The childhood rape still immobilizes me. I long for love, yet I resist. And when I'm alone I tremble with a knowing that rape will happen again." Caught in a terrible dichotomy of longing for a man's embrace but recoiling when it was offered, I feared I would never marry, let alone have children. Instead of looking at the painful dichotomy and asking God to help me walk in healing, I contented myself with holy language, such as "God has called me to be single forever. He *really* uses single people who have single-hearted devotion toward him. Yes, God is calling me to be a single missionary—just like the apostle Paul."

In retrospect I've come to see that God's healing is experienced in stages—as it was for the blind man in Bethsaida. There are times when I see things clearly and feel as if my heart is whole. There are other times when people look like trees, and I'm not so sure of my broken heart or myself.

In college the pieces of my life began to come apart like a giant jigsaw puzzle being tipped from a card table. It began when I shared too much of my upbringing with a guy I liked. Alarmed, he suggested I go to counseling. At that time I was surrounded by a group of people who thought counseling was the devil's work, so I chose to be holy and shun his advice. (Can you see the Pharisee in me?) People pointed me to the same verses I had already highlighted in my Bible— words about how God would give me everything I needed, how he would wipe away the past, how all I needed was his wisdom, not the foolishness of men.

During my first two years of college, I cried a lot—not really knowing why. Friends prayed for me, thankfully, and I slogged through. Real healing, though, came when God placed new friends in the path of my disintegrating life—friends who actually believed God would heal me. My first group of friends tried to tell me I was fine, that God had *already* taken care of my pain, and all I needed to do was walk in healing. But my new friends understood more clearly how God works. They saw the cracks in a life that looked fine on the outside but was crumbling internally. It wasn't until these friends showed me my broken heart and expressed their belief that God would repair it that I began to experience healing from the divine Heart Surgeon.

During my final two years of college, these friends laid their hands on me while I wept—deep, gut-churning sobs that came from places I'd abandoned. Silently, the Lord took me through many dark tunnels of healing. Each time I'd peer down a new tunnel and shudder. "Lord, why do you want me to walk in there? It's too dark."

"I'll be with you in the dark," he echoed in my mind.

"I don't like the dark. I've told you that before."

"Do you want to get well?" he asked.

"Well…er…uh." I'd list reasons why I couldn't possibly be healed. I'd point out that the past was the past and that I was all about the here and now. I congratulated myself on my forward thinking.

"Get up! Take up your mat and walk through the tunnel with me."

"But it's dark."

"Get up!"

Reluctantly I'd get up and follow him into the dark tunnel where fears from my past haunted me—fear of the night, fear of death, fear of abandonment, fear of relationships. Little by little, step by step, the Lord walked with me as I grieved. My friends prayed for me during my dark sojourns. I didn't realize it at the time, but grieving was a first step in moving from pain toward healing, both in my life and in my relationship with Jesus.

Each time I emerged from a tunnel of grief, I'd wipe red eyes, adjusting to the new vistas before me. I realized that I would never have seen the beautiful vistas on the other side had I not grieved in the dark tunnels with Jesus.

Like the blind man, I sometimes still see people as trees. Life can be blurry, but at least I see more clearly than I did in the past. I long for the day when my emotional healing is complete—when echoes of Jesus' laughter fill every part of me, when I hear the words, "Well done, good and faithful servant" (Matthew 25:23).

Twelve years after college I sat across from a counselor. I told her my story and expressed my reluctance to walk through even more pain and healing—this time so I could learn how to connect deeply with my husband and children.

"I don't understand it," she said.

"What?"

"With all you've been through, I'm surprised."

"Surprised at what?"

"That you are doing fine. You act as though you've been through years of therapy. You are sure you've never been to counseling before?"

I marveled at her words. Sitting across from her proved I wasn't averse to counseling. Still, I thanked God for the friends he had used to bring healing in my life when I was younger. I thanked him for the countless prayers they had prayed on my behalf—prayers that achieved the benefits of counseling. I thanked him for his steady hand in the darkness. When I heard the counselor's words, I knew my heart had been healed and was in the process of being healed by the Maker of all hearts.

WHY I LOVE THE STORY OF JOSEPH

But I am not completely whole. Frail, weary, impatient—all these characterize my life as a mother and a wife. However, I can thank God for things I wasn't able to thank him for in the past. Although I battle bitterness, I am slowly taking steps toward thanking God for my past—to be able to see that he placed me in my family of origin for a reason, that my past brought me to him, made me more like him.

It's because of the past that I have chosen to parent my children differently. By God's grace, I've examined my painful history, unearthing coping patterns that need to be replaced by healthier ones. True, my past has shaped me. But it doesn't have to determine how I parent my children. If I dare to yield to the God who revolutionizes lives, I can provide a secure home for my children.

Today, as a mom reading through my high-school and college journals, I am struck with how lonely I was and how desperate I was for a boyfriend. And then I envision how differently my daughters may respond to hormones and adolescence. I watch Sophie, poised and secure, able to love God. I see Julia not fretting about whether she has boyfriends but wrestling with God's calling on her life. By God's grace, my daughters have a more secure foundation than I had.

Mimicking the biblical Joseph, whose brothers sold him into slavery, I can say to the players of my past, "You intended to harm me, but God intended it for good to accomplish what is now being done, the saving of many lives" (Genesis 50:20). God has used my story. He led me "through the vast and dreadful desert, that thirsty and waterless land, with its venomous snakes and scorpions. He brought…water out of hard rock" (Deuteronomy 8:15).

While revisiting the past with my counselor, I again walked through dark tunnels, reliving long-forgotten memories. My husband, Patrick, told me, "I know your upbringing was hard. I want the last half of your life to be beautiful." God chose to bring Patrick into my life—a man who, more than any other person, has taught me about the love of Jesus. Though I was afraid, God made us one as we kissed at the altar. God replaced my "heroic" longing to be a single missionary and gave me the deepest desires of my heart—a family of my own. Though I have fretted I would mess up as a parent, he dared to entrust us with three grace-giving children.

Part of the beauty at the beginning of the second half of my life, though, has come through trials. Because God loved me so much, he chose to break me. But somehow his breaking has enlarged my capacity to experience him and share his love with others.

He did the same with Joseph:

God never uses anyone to a great degree until he breaks the person completely. Joseph experienced more sorrow than the other sons of Jacob, and it led him into a ministry of food for the nations. For this reason, the Holy Spirit said of him, "Joseph is a fruitful vine…near a spring, whose branches climb over a wall" (Genesis 49:22). It takes sorrow to expand and deepen the soul.[3]

Sold into slavery by his brothers, falsely accused of wrongdoing by a lustful woman, and imprisoned unjustly, Joseph walked through countless tunnels of healing with God. His past was painful, yet God chose him as a deliverer not just for his own clan but also for the world around him. He could have exacted revenge on his brothers, yet even in his weeping, he shunned bitterness. He lifted his eyes and looked beyond his brothers' treachery, able to thank God for using his awful journey to save many.

When Jesus asks, "Do you want to get well?" remember that he is not merely asking for your sake. As in Joseph's life, God's healing—his presence in darkness—is for the sake of delivering others for his glory. His healing trickles down into the lives you touch, especially those of your children. If you've never wanted to explore the darkness of your past and see God's light touch painful areas, choose to say yes to Jesus' question now. Jesus wants you to get well, and your children need you to. They need to hear the stories of hope woven uniquely by you.

How God Heals Us

If you've struggled through your upbringing, chances are someone pointed you to this verse: "I will repay you for the years the locusts have eaten—the great locust and the young locust, the other locusts and the locust swarm—my great army that I sent among you" (Joel 2:25). Although this verse was directed at the rebellious nation of Israel in exile, let's apply it to your situation of loss. The truth is that we all suffer—sometimes at the hands of others (locusts), sometimes as a result of our own sin, and always under the watchful eye of the Sovereign One. But the path to healing, in each situation, is the same.

As we walk through Joel 1 and 2, we see the locust verse in context and understand what God requires of us.

1. Acknowledge sin. Before God restores the years the locusts have gnawed, he asks us to acknowledge sin—not merely corporate sin but our own personal sins. "Put on sackcloth, O priests, and mourn" (Joel 1:13). Like Daniel, who acknowledged a nation's sin, God asks us to mourn both the sin of those around us and our own. It has been relatively easy for me to point my finger at people in my past, emblazoning others' mistakes on the movie screen of my mind. Yet, through it all, I forget that I have a log in my eye that is blinding me. For healing to occur, I must confess my own sin, and I must realize that I sin when I don't handle others' sins well. Sometimes I am so busy contemplating someone else's wrongdoing that I become embittered. That embittered attitude is just as much sin as the other person's initial offense.

2. Return to God. " 'Even now,' declares the LORD, 'return to me with all your heart, with fasting and weeping and mourning.' Rend your heart and not your garments. Return to the LORD your God, for he is gracious and compassionate, slow to anger and abounding in love, and he relents from sending calamity" (2:12-13). Those who suffered debilitating loss in childhood are either bitter or better. If they are better, it's because they've fallen headlong at the Savior's feet, imploring him for help. If they are bitter, they rail against God, blaming him for not rescuing them from the pain. The only way to experience the healing of God is to return to him. He is big enough to shoulder our questions, our angst, our bewilderment. But he cannot heal us if we stiff-arm him.

3. Don't be afraid of blessings and restoration. "Be not afraid, O land; be glad and rejoice. Surely the LORD has done great things" (2:21). Because of my up-bringing, I tend to view life pessimistically. Consequently, I don't let myself re-joice. Sometimes when things go well, I panic, expecting life to fall apart at any moment. When we bought our first house, I lay in bed that first night, worrying that a robber would break in or a fire would ignite and consume our home. When Sophie was born, I worried about every lurking disease.

In my pessimism, I am often *afraid* to be well. When Jesus asks, "Do you want to get well?" I shiver. I've spent many years coping with a difficult past, so I've become an expert at dealing with heartache. My problem now is *receiving* the good things God brings my way. Last night, while celebrating a friend's fortieth birthday, my children begged me to dance with them. I preferred to stay and talk with the grownups, but eventually my children's tears of disappointment rallied me. I danced with them. I celebrated. I reveled in the good things God has given me—my dear children. Dancing with clumsy feet, laughing with my chil-dren—this is what I want to learn to do. I don't want to be so comfortable cop-ing with grief that I forget to celebrate what's good.

4. Rejoice in God. "Be glad, O people of Zion, rejoice in the LORD your God, for he has given you the autumn rains in righteousness. He sends you abundant showers, both autumn and spring rains, as before" (2:23). God gives us so much. Yet, mired in pain, we can easily forget to remember him with rejoicing. Part of healing is learning the art of becoming glad. After you willingly let go of your fear of being made whole, take the next step and give yourself the grace to rejoice with nothing held back. God specializes in turning mourning into jitterbugging. Often I am so serious that my feet refuse his dance. Part of healing is *moving beyond* pain. God acknowledges both grief and joy, but he doesn't prize the former over the latter. Accept God's healing, and then rejoice fully in his grace and goodness.

5. Thank God for his Spirit. "And afterward, I will pour out my Spirit on all people. Your sons and daughters will prophesy, your old men will dream dreams, your young men will see visions. Even on my servants, both men and women, I will pour out my Spirit in those days" (2:28-29). If we are Christ followers, his Spirit lives within us. Even if the entire world turns its back on us, we are not alone. Even in darkness, the Holy Spirit is with you. Even when things go well, he is with you. Even if a friend turns her back on you, he is with you. Even when you hurt your spouse, he is with you. In every circumstance, every terror, every perplexity, the God of the universe has given you his Holy Spirit—to be with you.

6. Cultivate an eternal perspective. The end of the book of Joel talks about the *now* and the *not yet*. The *now* is God's promise to pour out his Spirit—the beautiful thing Jesus did after his life, death, and resurrection. The *not yet* is Jesus' return to earth in power:

> I will show wonders in the heavens
>> and on the earth,
>> blood and fire and billows of smoke.
> The sun will be turned to darkness
>> and the moon to blood
>> before the coming of the great and dreadful day of the Lord....
>
> Then you will know that I, the Lord your God,
>> dwell in Zion, my holy hill.
> Jerusalem will be holy;
>> never again will foreigners invade her. (2:30-31; 3:17)

Someday we'll turn our eyes, glassy from countless tears, to beyond the crystal sea where the King of kings and the Lord of lords sits on his throne. He will wipe away the tears, once and for all. He will no longer allow abandonment, violation, and sickness. We fail today. We mourn our losses. But a day will come when this life will be swallowed up and we will see with eternal eyes.

We will finally understand why our lives were so full of anguish. From earth we see the back of the tapestry God has woven, and it appears to be a knotted mess. With eyes of eternity, however, we'll understand the intricate woven pattern from God's vantage point. He selected the dark threads to bring dimension to our lives, to strengthen our character, to enlarge our capacity to love and serve him, to make us dependent on his strength. We may never see clearly in this life, but someday, in the light of eternity, we'll see clearly. We'll gaze at the front of God's tapestry, enjoying the glory of the artwork he created out of our lives—dark threads and all.

7. Tell your own story. Have you come to a place where you are tired of hearing people tell someone else's story? It's usually a dramatic success story, and if any struggle is mentioned, it becomes inconsequential compared to the person's tremendous victory. The struggle is minimized, if not negated entirely. It's one reason I am skeptical of some missionary biographies. The highlights and victories related there overshadow years and years of tumult and obscurity. Everyone's story is full of pain and praise, hardship and harmony.

I am telling my story in this book—a story of continued struggle in the midst of victory. From time to time, people ask me, "How do you hear from God? It seems like you are so close to him." When I tell them about the years of difficulty that brought me to an intimate place with Jesus, most people just shrug and walk away. There are many who don't want to be told that intimacy with the Savior often comes through painful journeys. They don't want to pay the price and walk through their own grief.

Still, Jesus asks us, "Do you want to get well?"

THE SAMARITAN WOMAN

Tired from a long day of ministry, dusty and thirsty, Jesus sat by a well. A Samaritan woman happened upon him. In the eyes of religious Jews in the first century, Samaritans were society's dregs. Yet Jesus asked the woman a question: "Will you give me a drink?" Taken aback that a Jew would stoop to ask her a question, she ventured into a discussion about Jews and Samaritans, wells and water. When Jesus spoke to her about living water, she asked where she could get it. Jesus inquired about her husband. After she told him that she had no husband, he recounted her past—every detail. Eventually, she spoke of the promised Messiah. Jesus, sitting across from her, said, "I who speak to you am he."

The woman, so enchanted by her meeting with Living Water personified, went back to town and said to her neighbors, "Come, see a man who told me everything I ever did." The Samaritans approached Jesus, and he, in turn, spoke his life-giving words to them. Later the townspeople pulled the woman aside and said, "We no longer believe just because of what you said; now we have heard for ourselves, and we know that this man really is the Savior of the world."[4]

As pioneer parents, we need to encounter Jesus. We need to be quiet enough to hear him tell our stories back to us in his resonant, grace-filled voice. We need to worship him in Spirit and in truth. We need to grieve, acknowledge sin, return, and rejoice. Once he has touched our lives and filled us with his living water, his love and amazing healing touch compel us to tell our stories to others, particularly our children.

"Come see Jesus. He knows everything about me, and yet he still gave me his living water," we tell our children. It is my sincere hope that my own healing story, knitted together with Patrick's, will cause our children to climb up on Jesus' lap. I pray that the One who heals me will heal them of the wounds I inflict. I desire to hear my children proclaim, "We no longer believe just because of what you said; now we have heard for ourselves, and we know that this man really is the Savior of the world."

Jesus will use your story in the same way with your children, if you will only let him.

"I Won't Become My Parents!"

Resisting the Urge to Make Destructive Vows

Let's decide not to become our mothers.
—BRANDY, a childhood friend

My friend Brandy and I had similar upbringings. We retreated to her room during her mom's spaghetti-flinging fights with her stepfather. We played elaborate make-believe games, pretending we were part of other families: She'd play Laura Ingalls, and I'd play Laura's sister Mary; we'd fight over who got to be Cindy Brady from *The Brady Bunch*. We both longed to have families like the ones we saw on television—intact, happy families where children were valued and parents solved conflicts amicably. We were too young to know that the shows on television didn't represent reality, but we weren't so naive as to think that our homes were stable. We longed for mothers who paid more attention to us. We pined after our fathers, who were divorced from our mothers.

Brandy and I hid under the covers when her mother and stepfather screamed obscenities and slammed doors. She reassured me when I worried that my mom would divorce for the third time. I listened when her mom divorced husband number two and then number three. From third to twelfth grade, we lived together through each other's upbringings.

UNWISE VOWS

"Let's make a promise, okay?" Brandy asked one lazy afternoon. We were twelve, I think.

"What promise?" I asked.

"Let's decide *not* to become our mothers. When we grow up, let's not make the same mistakes." Mostly, Brandy was talking about our mothers' penchant for smoking, but deep down her words resonated with me. I did not want to parent the way I was being parented. I didn't want my children to feel that they were unwanted or a mistake or in the way.

So, tucking Brandy's words away in a corner of my mind, I made a vow. *I will not parent the way I was parented.*

Vows can be a stimulus for positive change when the vow aligns with the pattern God is establishing in our lives. But a vow that is made to calm our fears, to bolster our confidence, to justify our anger, or to take upon ourselves the work that is really God's area of responsibility is a vow that will cause frustration and lead to defeat. Unfortunately, I speak from experience.

Everything Should Be Fine—Now That I've Paid My Dues

I remember making a vow to God during college. I didn't bother to check whether he agreed with my pact, but I made it nonetheless. My pact was this: I've had enough pain in my life from growing up. I don't need any more. Therefore, from this point henceforth, life should be easy. No pain. No trials. No problems with parenting. Nothing.

This became my impossible vow: *I will not have to experience new pain because I've had enough pain already.* I hoped the Lord would be amenable—that he'd see my logic—and acquiesce. But he didn't follow my agenda. For instance, there was my longed-for first pregnancy that ended with emergency surgery. As I shared earlier, on the way to the hospital, I yelled at God. "Now I *know* you don't love me," I sobbed. I couldn't believe God didn't accept my vow. He refused to reward my years of childhood pain by making my adult universe the way I wanted. Didn't he know that in order for me to fulfill that first vow—the one in which I swore I'd never become my mother—I needed to have children? Didn't he know I also needed a stress-free, happy life? What kind of God would allow my first baby to drop into my body cavity, away from the safe confines of my womb? After hours of surgery, I felt just like that sweet baby—detached from everything life giving.

I Won't Let Anyone or Anything Hurt Me

All this pain and my inability to deal with it led me to make another vow: *I will protect my heart at any cost.* If God can't take care of me the way I think he should, then I'll take control and never let anyone or anything hurt me again. This determination, although unspoken, made for an antiseptic approach to life. It also didn't make room for the strength of God. Instead of casting my fears of being hurt at his feet and asking him to help me, I steeled myself when pain came. With every fresh pain, I'd respond by constructing a wall around my heart.

A decade into our marriage, with three children in tow, Patrick recognized my wall, which by then had become like a Jericho fortress.

"You're detached," he told me.

"What do you mean?" Two things rose up in me: anger that he dared to point out my flaws and a seeping fear that I just might be found out.

"I feel like you've separated yourself from the family. I mean, I know you love us—it's just that you're hiding your heart."

I wanted to fight back, to insist his words weren't true, but I kept quiet, hoping I could keep the tears from coming. The weight of pain was so heavy, I was afraid if I dared let one tear escape, a torrent would follow. Somehow, I knew that if I let my pain out, I'd come undone.

In the midst of this conversation, I realized what my vows were costing my family. I understood that making vows like these could be harmful.

Perhaps you have made similar vows, thinking initially that you were declaring your allegiance to something God wanted for you. Or you might have made a vow despite the nagging suspicion that you were doing it to protect yourself or to try to control your circumstances or to attempt to block out pain.

It's wise to identify your vows, since it's possible to make a vow without realizing it. Once you have acknowledged the vows you have made, look carefully at each one to determine which ones are of God and which ones need to be discarded.

WHAT ARE VOWS?

A vow is often a statement of our determination to control an area of life. A vow frequently begins "I will never…" or "I will *always* be sure to…" A vow can be morally neutral: "I will brush my teeth morning and evening." "I will not allow the garbage can to overflow." A vow can be holy: "I take you, Patrick, to be my lawfully wedded husband." "Jesus, I give you my life." A vow can be destructive: "I will get even with him." "I will starve myself to stay thin."

The Bible speaks about vows, particularly in the Old Testament. Nazirites made vows that prohibited drinking alcohol and getting their hair cut. Israelites made financial vows to one another and to the Lord. These vows, if spoken, were binding, equal to a written contract today.

> If you make a vow to the LORD your God, do not be slow to pay it, for the
> LORD your God will certainly demand it of you and you will be guilty of
> sin. But if you refrain from making a vow, you will not be guilty. Whatever
> your lips utter you must be sure to do, because you made your vow freely
> to the LORD your God with your own mouth. (Deuteronomy 23:21-23)

In the New Testament, Jesus explained how important it is to mean what we say and say what we mean. He streamlined vow making:

> Again, you have heard that it was said to the people long ago, "Do not
> break your oath, but keep the oaths you have made to the Lord." But I tell
> you, Do not swear at all: either by heaven, for it is God's throne; or by the
> earth, for it is his footstool; or by Jerusalem, for it is the city of the Great
> King. And do not swear by your head, for you cannot make even one hair
> white or black. Simply let your "Yes" be "Yes," and your "No," "No"; any-
> thing beyond this comes from the evil one. (Matthew 5:33-37)

My husband follows Jesus' advice: If he says he'll do something, he does it. Once his face became purple when he mowed the lawn in 115-degree heat. Sure, the mowing lines were haphazard, but he finished the job because he said he would. That same type of determination, though, can be detrimental if we are following through on destructive vows. Hitler vowed to annihilate European Jews—and he nearly succeeded.

Keep in mind that I am not referring to positive life choices. Our vows to love our spouses and children as God directs and fulfill our responsibilities as pioneer parents can be a blessed springboard. We learn from what our parents did and didn't do. Making a conscious choice to parent differently while relying on the power of the Holy Spirit is different from making a vow based on our own stubborn determination.

Often we operate according to hidden vows whose existence we're not even aware of. These unvoiced vows sound something like this:

- No one will ever hurt me again.
- I will never trust a man (or a woman) again.
- I must earn love.
- I won't show my emotions.

When it comes to parenting our children, the vows sound a little different:

- I won't yell at my kids the way my father did or discipline my children harshly like my mother did.
- I'll be a stay-at-home parent so my children will know I love them.
- I won't allow poverty to touch my children's lives the way it touched mine.
- I will always be fun and spontaneous.
- I will make sure my children have more opportunities than I had.
- I will help my daughter become the basketball player I never was.
- My children will not be force-fed religion. They'll get to choose their own paths.
- I will make sure my children are raised in a highly structured Christian home.

All these vows, whether personal or parental, are reactions to pain or some missing element in our upbringing. All of them, on the surface, seem to be healthy responses. If something is broken, isn't it a good thing to fix it?

DESTRUCTIVE VOWS

It doesn't seem right to say that vows are destructive. Doesn't God want us to determine not to repeat the dysfunction of our parents? If we grew up in a home

environment we don't want to duplicate, how can we succeed unless we choose
to do the opposite?

The problem with making a vow isn't the wording. It's how the vow will be
fulfilled—typically by our own power—that makes the vow problematic. The
majority of the vows we make depend upon our strength and our ability to control the people and circumstances in our lives—not on God's ability to take care
of our hearts.

I love the feeling of satisfaction when I attain a goal I've set for myself. It
wasn't until I read the following words that I realized many of my vows were idol-
atrous: "In my commitment never to hurt again, I basically choose to worship an
idol—self-protection."[1]

The three vows that follow involve the idol of self-protection.

1. I will not parent the way I was parented. To be fair, the wording of this vow
is admirable. It shows my desire to parent my children differently. Yet this vow is
steeped in fear. I don't want to parent the way I was parented, because if I did,
my children would struggle to love me as I have struggled to love my mom. By
being the "perfect parent," I could eliminate the possibility that my children
would reject me.

2. I will not have to experience new pain because I've had enough already. When
I tell God I won't put up with any more pain and that he owes me a happy life,
I am taking it upon myself to educate *God* on what is moral and just. In an
attempt to protect myself, I seek to become the moral authority of the universe.
But he is God; I am not. Dictating to God what is acceptable pain in my life cir-
cumvents his authority.

3. I will protect my heart at any cost. If God can't take care of me the way I
think he should, then I'll take control and never let anyone or anything hurt me
again. This vow causes me to wall off my heart from my family—protecting me,
yes, but harming them. With the wall in place, I can't enter into my children's
pain. I lack empathy because I don't allow myself to feel uncomfortable emotions.
With the wall of self-protection chinked around my heart, I can't laugh and play.
If spontaneity might allow cracks in my wall, I withdraw.

When we make vows or continue to live according to past vows, it's an indication that we are still hurting. Whether we vow to be the opposite of our parents or become like them, we are still living in reaction to the past. I used to think

that parents who duplicate their own parents' mistakes hadn't dealt with their pasts and that those of us who determined to rise above the past were blessed survivors. Now I realize that *any* reaction to the past, whether positive or negative, whether making vows or morphing into our parents, is an indication that we need further healing.

How Can You Break Free?

Breaking free from vows you've made is not easy, but it *is* possible. God delights to heal us, particularly from burdens we take upon ourselves.

The one truth that has helped move me along the path of healing is this: *We do not have to protect ourselves. It's not our job.* As a child I did not feel protected. I had to rely on my wits and guts to keep safe. At that time I didn't know it was God's job to protect me and be with me. Now an adult, I still don't fully understand that truth. I still try to protect myself. Yet God waits with a hammer of grace—ready and able to take down the wall of self-protection that I've allowed to become an idol.

To break free from destructive vows, ask someone close to you who is a mature follower of Jesus to read this chapter. Then ask that person these questions:
- What vows do you think I've made?
- In what ways do you think I have tried to protect my heart?
- In what areas do you think I am parenting in my own self-determined strength?

Ask that friend to pray with you, to acknowledge the vows with you, and to help you hand them over to the Lord. You may want to ask a group of people to lay their hands on you and pray over you, asking God to set you free. Take several mornings or evenings to prayerfully journal your thoughts on the matter of vows. Have your spouse read your words and pray with you about your past injury.[2]

Making vows is living without God's help. The only way to break free is to seek help in the community of believers, to ask other Christians to come alongside you as you lay every burden and vow at the feet of Jesus and let him take them from you. You do not have to protect yourself. Let God have control. Let life throw its darts as you trust God to be there with you. Only God can free you from your past and enable you to parent your children with his grace, freedom, and beauty.

The End of the Story

The last time I saw Brandy, we were sitting together at our ten-year high-school reunion. The beautiful girl who'd been my unwavering confidante through a tumultuous upbringing was now in the throes of her own tumult. In high school I met Jesus under a towering evergreen tree, faith firmly taking root in the soil of my heart. But like the seed that fell among thorns and was choked (see Luke 8:5-8,11-15), even though Brandy had received Christ with vigor, the world's cares had strangled the vitality of her relationship with God.

At the reunion I noticed that her teeth were tobacco-stained and rotting. She looked weary, as if she carried the grief of someone much older, like she'd lived three lives. The vow we made came back to me then as she prattled on about her life as a waitress. Brandy had become her mother. Cutting herself off from Christ's healing, she walked the most familiar path.

It's only by grace that my children are growing up in a home different from the one I grew up in. Like Brandy, I have a natural tendency to fall back into the familiar. Like Brandy, I feel much older, as if I've lived three lives. And yet, because of God's surprising grace, he is doing something new in me. He's showing me the destructive vows I made. He's shedding light on my propensity for self-protection. And he's changing me, taking down my self-erected wall, brick by brick.

Recognizing destructive vows and letting them go will set you free to understand that, ultimately, it's God's responsibility to take care of you. In relinquishing control, you realize that an abundant life involves letting go of the tasks you've tried to take away from God, thinking you could do a better job than he can. To be set free, ask God to show you the destructive vows you have made. Ask a friend to pray with you as you let go of those vows. And then walk in freedom.

"What About the 491st Time?"

Forgiving Your Parents—Seventy Times Seven and Beyond

Forgiveness is giving up all hope of having a different past.
—UNKNOWN

Forgiveness. The word rolls off my tongue. If only bestowing it were as easy as saying it. Of all the paths I've walked, the road of forgiveness has been the most difficult. I remember my childhood in snapshots, often in black and white. I flip through photo memories in my mind.

Year one—my father smoking a pipe.

Year four—cracking and hoarding almonds at my grandparents' home.

Year seven—falling off my bike and ripping the flesh from my knee.

Year nine—smiling atop my horse, Epic.

Year ten—sitting stoically during my father's funeral, the end of my black-and-white memories.

I didn't understand forgiveness in the days of black-and-white memories. I only knew something wasn't right. I unfairly compared my thrice-divorced mom to a smiling Carol Brady in *The Brady Bunch* and also watched other families that were much healthier than my own. I was like a Dickensian waif peering through frosty windows, longing to be invited inside. I knew that my upbringing was not "normal."

It wasn't until I met Christ that the dilemma of forgiveness bounded into my life. Before that, I'd been happily bitter, nursing my anger as if it were an abandoned puppy in need of love. Life made sense that way. My parents hurt me; therefore, I had the right to be angry.

But Jesus changed things. For one, he changed my heart. Instead of having vengeful thoughts, I longed for my mother to come to know Christ. I soon realized I couldn't have this longing and hold on to my resentment. Something had to change. However, because I didn't recognize my own depravity and sinfulness—that would come later—I didn't fully appreciate Christ's forgiveness. I didn't understand that my sin placed the cross upon his sacred shoulders. Had I understood more fully what my sin did to Jesus, I would have been more apt to forgive those who had wronged me.

It wasn't until college, when a campus pastor challenged me to forgive my parents, that I realized how bitterness had taken over my life, my ambitions, and my relationships. Once I understood that, I determined to be the best little forgiver there ever was. I called my mom, hoping to extend grace. I asked her to forgive me for my lack of forgiveness. I forgave my father, even though he wasn't alive. Then I checked "forgive your parents" off the list and went on my "Mary way."

That was it. I had completed another discipleship step.

Many years later I still believed I had forgiven my parents. But when my daughter Sophie turned five, this simple event unleashed a torrent of emotion in me. Seeing her—so small, so vulnerable—brought back my five-year-old self in Technicolor. But now I was looking at the photo through new eyes, as a mother. In this new place, I had an even harder time understanding the behavior of my own mother. I became angry. I cried. I lamented. I thought I had forgiven her and everyone else from that era in my life. What was wrong with me? *Maybe I'm not really walking with God,* I thought. *If I can't forgive, what's wrong with me?*

It took a long time to understand that forgiveness is more than a one-time determination. It is a journey, a tumultuous, tortuous journey. We forgive not seven times but seventy times seven, as Jesus instructed. We have to have a lifestyle of forgiveness. Have I forgiven my parents? Yes and no. I've decided to, yes. But the process takes a lifetime, particularly if the person we long to forgive keeps on hurting us. Inevitably, though, forgiving those who have wronged us is the best gift we can give our children. It models the heart of Jesus to them. We are most like Jesus when we forgive.

What Forgiveness Is Not

As you and I embark on this reckless journey of forgiveness, we need to understand it more fully. To begin, we need to recognize what forgiveness is *not*.

1. It is not forgetting. When a memory seared my mind, I'd feel guilty. Why did I have to rehash past wrongs? Did that mean I hadn't forgiven, that I was walking in the sin of bitterness? Now, thankfully, I realize that I must remember in order to forgive. If I stuff my pain down deep, I'm only forgiving a mirage, a vapor. It's when the memory is fresh and monstrous that I can be like Jesus and utter, "Father, forgive them, for they didn't know what they were doing." *Remembering* is what makes forgiveness a revolutionary act. The reality of the scars makes the forgiveness an act of supernatural importance. If we gloss over the pain, we gloss over forgiveness, rendering it superficial.

Forgiveness also helps us reclaim what's good. For many years I could see only the pathological aspects of my upbringing. When I learned to forgive, I was able to remember the beautiful moments as well—memories that had eluded me when I'd dwelt on the darkness. Forgiveness was the light that scattered the darkness, and in its wake were good memories.

2. It is not a sign of weakness. Forgiveness is an indication of great strength and reliance on God. It is not weak to forgive. It's the most shocking, Kingdom-oriented act we can do. The Kingdom of God is a topsy-turvy, upside-down affair in which the weak are deemed strong, the poor are counted rich, the patient are applauded over the hasty. To the Enemy's camp, forgiveness is a vile act because it sets hearts free, hearts that Satan once shackled in bondage. That's what makes forgiveness an act of war against the prince of the power of the air.

3. It is not reconciliation. When my relationship with my mom failed to improve after my initial decision to forgive her, I used to worry that I hadn't really forgiven her. I equated forgiveness with reconciliation. But forgiveness is a one-sided act in which we choose to forgive another person. That person, though, has freedom to receive that forgiveness, shun it, pretend he or she doesn't need it, or insist nothing wrong was done worth forgiving. Reconciliation involves two people admitting their mutual sins and forgiving each other, whereas forgiveness involves only you. Romans 12:18 reminds us, "If it is possible, *as far as it depends on you,* live at peace with everyone."

4. It is not pretending that everything is fine or minimizing your anger. Sometimes we think forgiveness is downplaying our true feelings. If we can just sweep our rage under the rug, all will be well. It took me years to admit that I was really angry about my upbringing. Until I did that, I couldn't move forward with forgiveness, because prior to that, I had been forgiving an unreal past.

Similarly, forgiveness is not pretending all is well or glossing over someone else's sin against us. Pretending is something we do to escape reality. We pretend our spouse's hurtful remark didn't slice our heart. We pretend our child's door slamming doesn't bother us. The truth is, life is hard, and people hurt us. Pretending the world isn't that way won't eliminate the pain. If we spend our lives pretending things don't hurt, we won't be apt to take the first step onto the road to forgiveness. The more we pretend, the less we forgive.

5. It is not easy or superficial. Initially, when I "forgave" my parents and checked forgiveness off my list, I thought I was finished—that I could then move on to deeper spiritual things. Problem was, I was not finished with the process. For years I stymied God's redemptive reach in my life because I thought I had done all the forgiving I needed to do. I now know how desperately I need to breathe forgiveness every day.

Emotional and spiritual health depend on our willingness to engage in the process of forgiveness for the long haul. Even though our culture of avoidance has taught us to let bygones be bygones, avoiding the process of forgiveness is not a sign of spiritual maturity. Yes, we can work through conflict and deal with pain as it arises, but that is not the same as walking the path of forgiveness. It's a journey that takes years for God to peel away the many hidden layers of pain.

6. It is not painless. Forgiving those who have wronged us is painful. It involves remembering a debt, itself agonizing, and choosing to cancel that debt with joy. We retard the forgiveness process when we shy away from the pain of looking back. Remember, forgiving is not forgetting the pain and the sin that caused our pain. Forgiveness wouldn't be forgiveness if it were pain free.

What Forgiveness Is

As we continue this journey and seek to understand forgiveness more fully, we need to recognize what forgiveness *is*.

1. It is modeled and commanded by God. As I studied the biblical description of forgiveness, I found something that startled me. In the Old Testament, forgiveness is assigned only to God. You don't see people being commanded to forgive one another in the Old Testament, although it is implied. Instead, every reference to forgiveness refers to how God forgives his people.

> The LORD, the LORD, the compassionate and gracious God, slow to anger,
> abounding in love and faithfulness, maintaining love to thousands, and
> forgiving wickedness, rebellion and sin. (Exodus 34:6-7)

> O Lord our God,
>   you answered them;
> you were to Israel a forgiving God,
>   though you punished their misdeeds. (Psalm 99:8)

We rebel; God forgives. It is his nature. Throughout the Old Testament, we see the holiness of God interact with his mercy. His judgment is swift, yet his mercy and forgiveness are unrelenting. What's startling is how the idea that forgiveness is a divine act intersects the New Testament. The leaders of the first-century synagogue knew this fact: Only God can forgive sins. In the gospel of Mark, we see a paralyzed man being lowered through the roof of a home where Jesus was teaching. Jesus told the man, "Son, your sins are forgiven" (2:5). Notice how the teachers of the Law reacted: "Why does this fellow talk like that? He's blaspheming! Who can forgive sins but God alone?" (verse 7).

Jesus, of course, knew their thoughts. He replied,

> "Which is easier: to say to the paralytic, 'Your sins are forgiven,' or to say,
> 'Get up, take your mat and walk'? But that you may know that the Son
> of Man has authority on earth to forgive sins...." He said to the paralytic,
> "I tell you, get up, take your mat and go home." He got up, took his mat
> and walked out in full view of them all. (verses 9-12)

Forgiveness is a divine act; it is one holy proof of Jesus' divinity. What's stunning about Jesus is that he turns the tables on forgiveness by not only demonstrating it upon the cross but also requiring it of his followers. The New Testament is replete with his commands to believers that we must forgive others—even up to 490 times (70 times 7). If we claim to be Jesus' followers, we must emulate his life. Forgiveness is at the center of the Lord's Prayer: "Forgive us our debts, as we also have forgiven our debtors.... For if you forgive men when they sin against you, your heavenly Father will also forgive you. But if you do not forgive men their sins, your Father will not forgive your sins" (Matthew 6:12,14-15).

God the Father set the standard for forgiveness when he sent his only Son to earth. Jesus lived, breathed, and demonstrated forgiveness. If we call ourselves followers of Jesus, we must walk the earth as forgivers. Because the power and grace of God now reside in us through the Holy Spirit, we can dare to forgive.

2. *It is a lifestyle.* Bethany grew up in a home where lies were commonplace. "I remember we once came home from school and our dog was gone. Dad told us some story about a poor little handicapped girl who had been walking down our street. He felt sorry for her, so he gave her our dog. Later, at our neighbor's house, someone asked us about the animal-control truck that picked up our dog."

She battled unforgiveness, particularly when she married and had children. She describes the long journey she walked:

> The journey began when I decided to forgive my family for things they
> had done and not done. But then it took much inner healing through
> prayer, conferences, and good friends to process the pain from my child-
> hood. It's taken many years to figure out who needed forgiving, to decide
> to forgive, and to ask the Lord's help to forgive. It was not just a one-time
> deal for me, but a long process.

Although initially, forgiveness is a decision, it is better described as "a long process." Yes, we choose to release someone from our debt. That can take an instant. But learning to examine and understand our reactions to a painful incident takes a lifestyle of forgiveness.

3. *It is continual and layered.* Because we live in a fallen world, we'll have to forgive again and again. Jesus said, "If your brother sins, rebuke him, and if he repents, forgive him. If he sins against you seven times in a day, and seven times comes back to you and says, 'I repent,' forgive him" (Luke 17:3-4).

Forgiveness is layered. As wind and rain strip away the layers of peeling paint on a house, God uses the weather of our lives to expose old paint, layer by layer. In college, when I "forgave" my parents, I was staring at the pristine top layer of forgiveness. Years later I've had the agony and joy of seeing more layers peeling off, each representing something more to forgive. Perhaps the greatest joy of heaven will be that the paint will be blessedly power-washed off. Those who sinned against us will be clean, and we will be cleansed from our sins against others as well.

4. It is freeing. Remember playing the game in gym class in which everyone stands holding hands in a circle, and then kids crisscross the circle until the entire group is in a hopelessly knotted mess? Often, getting knotted is the easy part; it's the unwinding and stepping over and under people that is difficult. Forgiveness is that process. We have to step in and out of memories, under people who have wronged us, over people we've wronged, until we're no longer knotted. The only way to do that is through forgiveness. And once we've decided to forgive, the knots of our lives begin to unravel.

Forgiveness helps us realize that none of us gets parenting right. We all fail. Our grandparents failed. Our parents failed. We fail. Our children will fail. Jesus can free us from a hardened heart if we forgive our parents. He can unshackle our propensity to wallow in our own sin because he forgives us. The more we live a lifestyle of continual forgiveness, the more grace we will offer our parents, who need grace just as much as we do.

5. It is the antithesis of bitterness. Bitterness is the decision to hold others accountable for their sin, to nurse the pain, to desire to inflict injury. With bitterness comes bondage, because the more I consider the offenses of others, the more I am tied to the past and not living in the present. I've clutched bitterness to my heart as if it were the lone chocolate bar on a deserted island. Once I let go of the bitterness—something I have to do daily—I experience great freedom because I finally let God be God. He is the Disseminator of Justice. When I insist on clinging to bitterness, I take his place. When I let go of bitterness, I give him free reign.

The author of the book of Hebrews cautioned against bitterness. "See to it that no one misses the grace of God and that no bitter root grows up to cause trouble and defile many" (12:15). If we have bitter, unforgiving hearts, we miss the grace of God. We become troubled, defiled. But forgiveness does just the opposite: It makes us joyful recipients of God's grace.

6. It is an indication of the depth of our relationship with God. If we don't grant forgiveness to our parents, then we don't *really* understand Jesus' sacrifice for our sins. Jesus told a pointed story about the unmerciful servant. A king forgave a servant a whole bucketload of debt—millions of dollars—after he begged and pleaded with the king. The servant was relieved, but he didn't really understand the great debt he had been forgiven. He went out and found a man who owed him a few dollars and told the man to pay him back immediately. The man pleaded for mercy, but the servant had the man thrown in jail.

The king called the servant in and said, "You wicked servant...I canceled all that debt of yours because you begged me to. Shouldn't you have had mercy on your fellow servant just as I had on you?" (Matthew 18:32-33).

We've been forgiven an immense debt—our millions of sins against a holy God. Yet when we fail to forgive the hundreds of sins our brother or sister has committed against us, we show how little we really understand God's profuse forgiveness. The more we internalize his forgiveness, the more we will grant it to those who have wronged us.

7. It is seeing the past as a gift. Because Jesus' forgiveness invigorates our forgiveness, we can view the past as a period of time Jesus used to bring us to himself. Having a difficult childhood can actually be considered a blessing. How? Because from an early age we learned we couldn't live life on our own. Chances are, the very instability of a childhood home drove you into the arms of the Changeless One. So, in an indirect way, God uses our parents' failures to draw us deeper into his embrace. The beauty of forgiveness is that when we *do* remember our stories, God redeems and reinterprets them for his glory. As we forgive others, we can eventually thank him for the past.

8. It is costly. The ultimate price Jesus paid to secure our forgiveness tells us that the process of forgiveness is never easy. It's painful to remember injury. Sometimes when we remember the past, we uncover festering wounds. When Jesus cleans and binds our wounds, we cry out in pain. The wounds of the past will never be healed, though, unless we go through the painful process of uncovering them before the eyes of the Forgiving One.

Dietrich Bonhoeffer said, "Forgiveness is the Christ-like suffering which it is the Christian's duty to bear."[1] Just as forgiveness cost Jesus his life, forgiveness costs us. Forgiveness is ever costly, ever painful.

9. *It is a recognition of our own need.* Scott grew up in a home with an emotionally absent father (who later took his own life) and a critical mother. Scott's journey of forgiveness began when he understood his own need for it. "As an adult, you come to realize that your parents are sinners who need forgiveness and peace with God (just like you do). You come to appreciate that they, too, were shaped by their environment (just like you were). You figure out that they weren't perfect (just like you). And you either cower from them or get mad at them, or you forgive them so that you can move on in your life."

The journey of forgiveness is cluttered with muddy ruts and glorious vistas. As a pioneer parent raising your own children, you will find no easy prescription for forgiving your parents for the pain they caused you. It requires reliance on the Holy Spirit, a desperate longing to be whole, and relinquishing your agenda to harm those who harmed you.

Since we are most like Jesus when we forgive, a primary tenet of our parenting must be forgiveness. We must model his forgiveness and extend grace to our children. We must forgive their grandparents. Our lives should be an inviting portrait of Christ—of his death, burial, and resurrection—all of which demonstrated forgiveness.

"It's Time to Leave Home"

Leaving the Nest; Clinging to Your Spouse

Happiness is having a large, loving, caring,
close-knit family in another city.
—GEORGE BURNS

I'm not sure if I thought of Adam and Eve when I walked teary-eyed down the aisle toward Patrick, my soon-to-be husband. I should have.

God set out a simple plan for marriage in the second chapter of Genesis: "For this reason a man will leave his father and mother and be united to his wife, and they will become one flesh" (verse 24). Jesus reiterated this same design in Matthew 19:5, as did the apostle Paul in Ephesians 5:31. It is interesting to note that God uttered this holy suggestion before Adam and Eve chose to disobey him. They were distinctly human yet unstained by sin; therefore, God's design for us to leave our families of origin and become one in marriage is of the highest significance. We are fulfilling his amazing mandate, representing humankind in its sinless state, when we leave home and unite ourselves to our spouses.

The marriage covenant is not to be taken lightly; it is a representation of God's redemptive plan. The apostle Paul described the church's relationship to Christ as a marriage. A troubled marriage, then, fails to present to the world an accurate picture of the relationship between Christ and the church. The world needs to see the marriage covenant being lived out—a living, breathing example of God's ideal, the culmination of his instructions to the first man and woman in a perfect garden. However, to live out this ideal, we must first unpack what it means to leave and unite.

The *New American Standard Bible* uses words such as *leave* and *cleave*. We are to leave our families of origin and cleave to our spouses. *Leave* is translated from the Hebrew word *'azab,* which means "to relinquish, let go of, loosen, set free, or depart from." *Cleave* is taken from the Hebrew word *dabaq,* which means "to cling, adhere, follow closely, catch, or pursue."

So, put simply, in marriage

- we relinquish the hold our parents have over us and cling to our spouse;
- we let go of our parents' influence and adhere to our spouse's desires;
- we break out of the grip of our parents' expectations and follow closely the needs of our spouse;
- we set ourselves free from our parents' hopes and catch our spouse's hopes for the future; and
- we disembark from our parents' home to create a new home with our spouse.

Easier said than done. Leaving home and establishing your own family unit is a difficult task.

In the bird kingdom, this leaving happens abruptly. A mother stirs her nest, making it prickly and uncomfortable for her baby birds. Then, without so much as an "I'll miss you," she kicks them out, sending them fluttering into the foreign air on unsteady wings.

In the human kingdom, the opposite is true. Some mothers and fathers have a hard time stirring the nest. Sometimes they remodel the nest, making it so attractive that children return as adults and take up emotional residence there. Then, when this emotionally dependent child marries, the marriage becomes divided because the child has one foot in the parents' nest and another in his or her own. Yet God tells us to grow up, to leave our families of origin physically and emotionally, and to cling to our new families.

I speak from experience. Patrick and I have been leaving our families every year of our marriage in different ways and on different levels. We are still learning what it means to cleave to each other.

For us it started on our wedding day—the day I daydreamed about as a little girl. Wearing white, filled with hope and blessed anticipation for a new life, I smiled through my veil at the thought of being Patrick's wife. Since we decided to have our pictures taken before the service, the photographer arranged for us to have our moment together when I walked down a ribbon-draped aisle toward Patrick. A flurry of snapshots ensued, and we began the process of shifting people and family members on stage. When it came time for Patrick's parents to stand with us, they refused. So broken were they by our decision to be married in a Protestant church, they couldn't bring themselves to stand at the altar to have their picture taken.

Don't cry. Don't cry, I commanded my tear ducts. But they disobeyed. I sobbed on my wedding day, not from elation, but from disappointment. It was a stark beginning for us—the beginning of leaving our families. We had made choices Patrick's parents didn't like, particularly about where we chose to worship God. It broke their hearts. And yet we moved forward, deeply saddened that his parents were disappointed in us.

A few years later we had an epiphany of sorts. After a series of confrontations with his family, Patrick stood up for me, indicating that he would not allow his family to continue treating me in such an antagonistic way. Eventually, by God's grace, we reconciled with his parents. They no longer confront us on our choice of churches, and we try not to reopen the wound. The process of leaving his family, though, has been excruciating. Because his parents continue to be injured by our choices, it is difficult for us to talk about what is most important to us: Jesus.

Eight years into our marriage, we moved across the country, physically leaving both our families behind. I thought I'd left mine already. It wasn't until I saw my family of origin from a distance that I realized I had yet to *emotionally* unglue myself from them. There are two signs that indicate you have not emotionally left your family:

1. You mull over your conversations with your parents continually, worrying about what you said and what you could have said differently.
2. You choose never to think about the family you grew up in, believing, "That's my past. It's over. I'm fine."

I was the mulling type. One memory came back to me during this time that typified an emotional connection I was still making to my extended family. I was probably fifteen years old. My grandmother wanted my family to arrive at her house first thing on Christmas morning. My mom didn't want to get up that early, especially considering that we had to feed our horses, then drive an hour to my grandmother's house. I wanted to please my grandmother so much that I set our clocks forward one hour. When I told my grandmother what I'd done, it became part of family lore—one of those proud stories told over and over amid laughter. I didn't realize how entrenched I was in pleasing my family and how pathetic my actions were until I had some emotional distance.

Patrick and I experienced a second honeymoon of sorts when I began to emotionally leave my family, but it took thousands of miles of separation for me to make the decision. A part of my heart still cried for parental and grandparental approval. A part of me was still the little girl asking, "Do you love me?" As long as I remained shackled to that neediness, I was not aligned with Patrick. To make him a priority, I had to leave my family. When they wanted my allegiance, I had to start elevating my marriage.

Last year I realized that my emotional ties to my family of origin were not only bad for my marriage, but they also inhibited my relationship with Jesus. Jogging through my neighborhood, I prayed the prayer I'd breathed nearly every day: "Lord, please help me love my mother more."

His still, small voice whispered, "Mary, your problem isn't that you love your mother too little, but that you love her too much."

"Really?"

"Yes. You value her opinion and approval of you more than my opinion and approval of you." I'm still wrestling with God's words. In that wrestling, I've realized that following Jesus will cost me the human approval I crave. It will cost aspects of my relationship with my family, particularly because they don't understand my relationship with Jesus.

Why Leave?

If leaving your father and mother behind is so problematic, why bother? Didn't God create that family? Doesn't he want you to honor your father and mother?

The Christian life is replete with such paradoxes—dual contrasting truths that God intends us to hold in tension rather than adhere to one side of the paradox while ignoring the other. Yes, we must honor our parents, but not in a way that dishonors God or our spouses. Yes, we must take care of our parents. To deny that would make us Pharisaical, appearing to love God yet neglecting members of our families who are in need. But we must not allow our parents' opinions to influence us when their views conflict with what God wants.

Consider the following four reasons to leave your family of origin and cleave to your mate.

1. We leave and cleave to follow God's Kingdom. In our culture, it doesn't often cost us in human relationships when we follow God's call. In other countries, however, following Jesus often means the loss of parental relationships. In some Muslim countries, it is against the law to convert to another religion. Parents of children who convert sometimes turn them in to the authorities. Some Hindu parents in India kick their converted children out into the streets and never talk to them again. The cost of following Christ and living for his Kingdom is high. Although we may not experience such a severe reaction from our parents, if they aren't living for the Kingdom of God, we will experience plenty of conflict and pain.

God calls us to leave everything and everyone to follow him. Consider Jesus' harsh Kingdom words:

> If anyone comes to me and does not hate his father and mother, his wife
> and children, his brothers and sisters—yes, even his own life—he cannot
> be my disciple. (Luke 14:26)

> Peter said to him, "We have left all we had to follow you!"
> "I tell you the truth," Jesus said to them, "no one who has left home
> or wife or brothers or parents or children for the sake of the kingdom of
> God will fail to receive many times as much in this age and, in the age to
> come, eternal life." (Luke 18:28-30)

We should endeavor to leave our families, if that is God's call, for the sake of living with an eternal perspective. Jesus promises us that the heartache we experience on this side of heaven will be rewarded, and we will be comforted.

Is it any surprise that we'll be persecuted, even by members of our own families? The apostle Paul asserted that "everyone who wants to live a godly life in Christ Jesus will be persecuted" (2 Timothy 3:12). Persecution is a matter of daily life if we are Kingdom seekers. Jesus' family and friends "took offense at him. But Jesus said to them, 'Only in his hometown and in his own house is a prophet without honor.' And he did not do many miracles there because of their lack of faith" (Matthew 13:57-58). Jesus knew well the rejection of those he loved.

I used to believe the lie that it was up to me to save my extended family. I worried when Patrick and I moved thousands of miles away. I thought, *How can they come to know Christ without me?* I failed to realize that Jesus' own family came to believe in him later, not when he spent time in his hometown. The God of the universe is big enough to save our families, even when we venture far away. Maybe God wants you to move away *so that* he can redeem your extended family. Maybe God wants you to move away so that he can have your full allegiance and so that you can learn to cling to your spouse.

2. We leave and cleave to show our allegiance to our spouses. We leave our families and cleave to our spouses because God commands it. Even if you're unmarried, the principle remains the same. We must grow up, leave home, and make a life for ourselves. In terms of marriage, though, if we are constantly running to our parents or elevating our parents above our spouses, our marriages will suffer and, ultimately, our children will bear the consequences.

Suzanne didn't realize her emotional connection to family had such an unhealthy influence on her marriage. "I just left my family a year ago, and we've been married nine years.... The Lord has revealed my connection to my family of origin as sin. Now I know my family to be those who live under the same roof as I do. They are my priority. Then come those who share bloodlines with me or my husband."

Jack admits to having similar issues: "It was not until year four of our marriage that I made a conscious decision not to ride the fence between my mom and my wife. It was a difficult decision; it meant going against everything I had ever known. It meant defying the one no one defies. It was the turning point for our marriage."

In a traditional marriage vow, we utter the phrase "forsaking all others" without really knowing what that means. I used to think it meant that we wouldn't be close friends with people of the opposite sex. Now I realize it means *anyone* who takes a priority over a spouse. That sometimes means our parents. I remember the day I made a conscious choice to choose my husband over my family. I incurred their wrath and disapproval, and I mourned.

Oddly, in the midst of the sadness of realizing my family put conditions on their love, I felt incredible joy. So did Patrick. He said, "Thank you for loving me. Thank you for choosing me." Choosing Patrick over the whims of my family helped redeem and establish our marriage.

3. We leave and cleave to unshackle ourselves from expectations. Other people's expectations can smother our spirits. Add parental expectations to the mix, and you have a recipe for stagnation. Truth be told, we will never meet our parents' expectations. The key to overcoming oppressive parental expectations is to leave, giving those expectations an extended holiday.

Freedom came—and is still coming—when I realized who my audience was. It was not my parents. It was not my children. It was not the other parents in the world who seemed to parent their children perfectly. It was not even my husband. Jesus is my audience, the Audience of One. When we leave our families of origin, we are taking one more step toward the ovation of heaven.

4. We leave and cleave to grow up. A baby bird will never learn to fly if its mother doesn't push it out of the nest. We will never learn to fly as adults if we are tied unhealthily to our parents—their money, their approval, their control. To grow up is to establish an independent household, to become fiscally responsible, to make adult decisions about how we will parent our children. If we don't separate our souls from our parents, we are more apt to repeat their mistakes.

How Do You Leave?

If you are convinced that God commands you to elevate your marriage and break emotional entanglements with your parents, then you're ready to leave. But how do you get disentangled from your family of origin so you can cleave to your spouse? Following are four essential steps you must take to leave your parents.

1. You must leave physically. Living within the framework of *Everybody Loves Raymond* is unhealthy for everyone involved. You may not have a meddlesome Marie Barone living across the street, stopping by regularly to lay a mother-in-law guilt trip on you. But even if you live hundreds of miles away from your parents and still value your mother's (or your mother-in-law's) opinion over your spouse's, get ready for marital turmoil. Fans of *Everybody Loves Raymond* laugh at the sitcom because it's true to life for so many families. But don't let it be true for you, whether your parents live across the street or across the continent.

I know daughters who run to Daddy for money when things get financially tight. I know men who are emasculated by their wives' constant communication with their fathers. I know women who anguish over their husbands' connection with their mothers. So don't doubt this truth: We must leave.

Sometimes leaving is literal and physical, requiring geographical distance to be inserted between you and your parents. Or it might mean making choices to not rely on your parents for financial assistance. The more our parents are tied to us, the more control they have over our choices.

It is imperative for us as pioneer parents to separate from our parents for the sake of our children. If we want to raise our children in a different environment, we must cut the ties to old, dysfunctional patterns. For Patrick and me, that meant establishing boundaries around our marriage. It also meant moving away.

2. You must leave emotionally. Leaving emotionally is messy. It takes time. It takes introspection and prayer. Sometimes it takes counseling. In order to emotionally leave your family of origin, you must dare to look back. Therapists Don and Jan Frank give this freeing advice: "One of the best ways of dealing with your history so that you can get beyond it is to walk through a grieving process. Grieving is simply pouring out your heart to God and others."[1]

I've had to uncover painful memories, live a lifestyle of forgiveness, and ask the Lord for grace to fill my heart. The only way I've been able to break free of my family's influence is through other people's prayers and through my husband's patience.

3. You must leave spiritually. Particularly for pioneer parents, an essential part of leaving involves leaving spiritually. We cannot hope to impart spiritual truth to our children if we are confused about what the truth is. We need to own our spirituality, to know Jesus personally, to experience him as Lord and Savior, regardless of our parents' opinions and religious practices—or lack thereof. This is one area of leaving that Patrick and I have been able to do successfully, particularly because we held firmly to our beliefs, starting with the location of our wedding ceremony. As a result, we've experienced little interference from our parents in the way we raise our children in the Christian faith.

4. *You must view cleaving as a* good *thing.* After we leave our families of origin, we need to replace the leaving with cleaving. If we don't, our marriages will suffer.

Oneness was the perfect design that God announced in the Garden of Eden, and it is still God's design today. Oneness is assailed on many fronts. Often, men and women both work outside the home, increasing the potential for isolation. The enemy of our souls works overtime to create discord, bitterness, and strife. Our own unmet expectations become a barrier to oneness. Our selfishness, wanting only our own desires fulfilled, desecrates oneness. The handling (or mishandling) of money creates division. Our maleness and femaleness and the subsequent gender perspectives encumber unity. Poor communication, especially for pioneer parents who didn't grow up with healthy ways of handling conflict, divides spouses.

At a marriage conference, Patrick and I heard this beautiful statement: "Our right perspective of God and his character allows us to receive our mate as God's perfect provision for us."[2] To cleave to each other, we must first cleave to the Lord. Knowledge of his perfect character and his unconditional love is the basis for accepting and clinging to our mate.

When Patrick and I were paddling through some rough waters in our marriage, I tended to nag and whine and force him to become what I wanted him to be. Instead of bringing us to oneness, these actions pushed him farther away. The Lord indicated I should spend time hearing his voice, obeying whatever he told me. It was only when I took my eyes off my husband's supposed faults that I was able to see my own. Concentrating on the Lord showed me my own sin. Adoring the Lord eventually led me to adore Patrick. Accepting each other as God's perfect gift based on God's merit has helped us tremendously in our cleaving journey.

In the Garden of Eden, God stated the importance of leaving both father and mother in order to cling fast to each other, to start a new family. This wisdom is essential to our success as pioneer parents. We have the Holy Spirit residing within us, and he gives us the power to obey God by leaving and cleaving. Even so, there is no guarantee that our earthly parents won't forsake us, ridicule us, or turn their backs on us. For the sake of our children, though, we must not ignore God's design. We must leave our parents so that we can parent our children in a new way.

"But My Parents Drive Me Crazy"

What It Means to Honor Your Parents

Honor your father with all your heart,
and do not forget the mother who created you.
—RABBI BEN-SIRA

The Texas Ten Commandments are painted on the wall of an East Texas church. Number five reads, "Honor yer Ma and Pa." It's a simplified version of the biblical commandment, but obeying it is not as simple as it sounds. As pioneer parents, we hope to honor our mothers and fathers who may have dishonored us, and we want to instill honor in our own children.

In the previous chapter, we looked at God's command to leave and cleave. God commanded us to honor our parents *and* to leave them, so we must accept the notion that leaving and honoring can happen simultaneously.

I've struggled with the idea of honor ever since I breathed my first prayer to Jesus. How do I honor parents who dishonored me? How do I love and hold in high regard people who have little regard for Jesus?

THE JEWISH CONCEPT OF HONOR

Honor is a core biblical concept. But what does it mean? The Hebrew word for "honor" is *kabbed,* the verb found in the fifth commandment. This word means "to be heavy or weighty, to give weight to, to assign importance to, to be honored." It is tied to a parent's position, not to his or her personality. We are to give weight to the honorable *position* that our parents hold.

Ben-Sira, a Jewish rabbi who wrote Old Testament commentary, said this about honoring the position of our parents: "Honor your father with all your heart, and do not forget the mother who created you. Remember that you came from them—and what can you give like that which they have given you?"[1] Our parents gave us life; therefore, they are due honor. First-century Jewish historian Philo expanded upon this idea. Children of all ages "are to honor, respect, fear, and obey those who gave them life, and to care for parents in their old age as they themselves were cared for in their youth." To fail in doing so is not only a breach of human trust but also an affront to God, "for parents are the servant of God for the task of begetting children, and he who dishonors the servant dishonors also the Lord."[2]

Honor, then, is an attitude of graciousness and thankfulness toward our parents for the roles they've played in our lives. Regardless of the hurtful things they've done, God chose them to be our parents, and they are due honor. We must be courteous and kind to them. In addition, there is strong evidence that honor includes taking care of our parents when they become infirm or aged. Jesus called the Pharisees hypocritical for acting religious while neglecting their parents:

> And why do you break the command of God for the sake of your tradition? For God said, "Honor your father and mother" and "Anyone who curses his father or mother must be put to death." But you say that if a man says to his father or mother, "Whatever help you might otherwise have received from me is a gift devoted to God," he is not to "honor his father" with it. Thus you nullify the word of God for the sake of your tradition. You hypocrites! (Matthew 15:3-7)

But what about honoring parents who were ungodly? In rabbinic literature, this is called the problem of the wicked father. It doesn't allow for youths to simply declare, "I have the problem of the wicked father, so now I can dishonor him." Even when a father or mother is "wicked," a child still must show honor. And if the child needs to correct his or her father, it must be done without condescension.

If a parent tells us to do something contrary to God's law, what are we to do? Obey God first. Jewish scholars concur: "We recall that the reverence and service owed a father is superseded by the reverence and obedience owed by both father and son to God: the father who demands immoral or impious behavior of his son is to be disobeyed."[3] It is always our responsibility to honor God first.

The Look of Honor

In his sovereignty, God chooses to place people in specific families (see Psalm 68:6). We may never fully understand his reasons this side of heaven. Yet the most freeing thing I've discovered is that God set me in my family for his purpose. Whether you had the most nurturing home or the most abusive one, God gave you your parents; therefore, you must endeavor to give them honor.

Before you despair, consider how Jesus honored his parents. What you discover may surprise you.

Jesus' Obedience Cost His Mother and Father
As a boy, Jesus was subject to his parents. Yet at age twelve, he chose to obey his heavenly Father rather than his earthly stepfather by staying behind at the temple to discuss matters of Scripture with the teachers of the Law. He made provision for Mary in his death, but it was his obedience to the Father that made him leave her in the first place.

One truth that is hard to accept is that sometimes our obedience to the Father will cost our parents. Oswald Chambers acknowledged this hard truth:

> If we obey God it is going to cost other people more than it costs us, and that is where the sting comes in. We can disobey God if we choose, and it will bring immediate relief to the situation, but we shall be a grief to our

Lord. Whereas if we obey God, he will look after those who have been pressed into the consequences of our obedience. We have simply to obey and to leave all consequences with him.[4]

Jesus Brought a Sword That Separates Relationships
Jesus told his disciples,

> Do not suppose that I have come to bring peace to the earth. I did not come to bring peace, but a sword. For I have come to turn "a man against his father, a daughter against her mother, a daughter-in-law against her mother-in-law—a man's enemies will be the members of his own household." Anyone who loves his father or mother more than me is not worthy of me. (Matthew 10:34-37)

There is much confusion about what Jesus' words mean. Isn't he the Prince of Peace? Didn't the angels proclaim peace on earth when the infant Jesus uttered his first cry? Yes, Jesus came to bring peace between God and humanity. He justified us by taking our sins upon himself and suffering the punishment we deserved. Because of his sacrifice, we have amazing peace with God.

That same peace, however, causes division between people. Jesus draws a line in the sand between those who follow him and those who don't. That line is sometimes drawn right down the middle of a family, making our parents "enemies." Does that let us off the hook? Should we then write them off because Jesus said they're our enemies?

Consider what Jesus said about how we should treat enemies:

> But love your enemies, do good to them, and lend to them without expecting to get anything back. Then your reward will be great, and you will be sons of the Most High, because he is kind to the ungrateful and wicked. Be merciful, just as your Father is merciful. (Luke 6:35-36)

Go ahead! If your parents oppose you, treat them like enemies.

HONORING GOD, HONORING PARENTS

To understand honor, place it within the context of first-century Palestine, where a person's identity was seldom thought of in any individual sense. Rather, identity was defined in connection with a family, a trade or vocation, or a location. Jesus' disciples James and John were identified as sons of Zebedee. Joseph, Jesus' stepfather, was a carpenter. Jesus himself was often connected with his hometown, Nazareth.

For Jesus to say we are to love him more than our actual family identity is surprising. The same God who told us to honor our mother and father also said that his Son came to divide families. Harsh but true.

What then does it mean to honor our parents if they do not honor Christ? The key to honor is to first honor Jesus, realizing that this act may be the very thing that alienates you from your family. No one ever said discipleship is easy. Before we are daughters or mothers, before we are sons or fathers, we are primarily followers of Jesus Christ. Jesus should have our highest allegiance, our deepest affection. Dietrich Bonhoeffer said it well: "When Christ calls a man, he bids him come and die."[5]

So how do we honor our parents? If we follow Jesus, it will mean holding our relationships loosely, realizing that our true brothers, sisters, fathers, and mothers are those who share our faith. Jesus demonstrated this truth in the following exchange:

> Then Jesus' mother and brothers arrived. Standing outside, they sent
> someone in to call him. A crowd was sitting around him, and they
> told him, "Your mother and brothers are outside looking for you."
> "Who are my mother and my brothers?" he asked.
> Then he looked at those seated in a circle around him and said,
> "Here are my mother and my brothers! Whoever does God's will is my
> brother and sister and mother." (Mark 3:31-35)

With Jesus' words as a backdrop, how do we follow his example as we try to honor our parents in daily life?

1. *Tell the truth.* Jesus *is* the truth, and he honored people by telling the truth and giving them the opportunity to repent. Why is it that we tend to shy away from truth?

Telling the truth in a loving and kind way is the most freeing thing we can do as we honor our parents. I lived in a shame-based family system. Few family members told the truth. Most embraced half-truths—that is, until we expressed our *real* feelings by gossiping behind people's backs. One of the most difficult things I've had to do (and am still learning to do) is to not shy away from telling the truth to my extended family. I've shared Christ with them on many levels, but I've had a hard time telling them when their words or actions hurt me.

Once I told my mom that her words about my lack of exercise hurt me. "It makes me feel like I am a wimp, like you don't value me because I'm not in the same shape you are. It's enough for me just to keep the house clean and the family fed. Please stop mentioning my lack of physical exercise." As a result, I was no longer in knots about my mom's words. I was able to forgive her once I brought my grievance into the light. As a side benefit, she didn't pester me about it again. Oddly, two years later I competed in a triathlon! Telling her the truth about this small thing was honoring to her, especially since I told it for the sake of forgiving her. It gave her the opportunity to repent and helped her see how she could love me better.

Jillian wrestles with truth and honor. "How do I honor a father who never calls me, who lives as a con artist?" It may be that your parents are unable to tell the truth. Or, like Jillian, you may have a chronic swindler for a father. Still, it is important to tell the truth, even when your parents won't hear or absorb it. For their sakes—to honor them—you must speak the truth in love. If you pretend that everything was and is well, you do your parents a disservice. When Jesus told the truth, he did so in a way that invited repentance and restoration. Our job is to tell the truth in the same spirit, with an eye toward our parents' redemption. Telling the truth and honoring our parents act in tandem.

Suzanne, who grew up with an absent mother and an emotionally distant father, wrote poetry to share the truth with her parents. She sent her poetry to them with an eye toward redemption, not in an effort to hurt or malign them. "For my parents to read the poems poured onto a page by a weeping poet was quite a shock," she says, "an emotional defibrillation they needed to get their hearts going again.… We share honestly now, more honestly than I have ever shared with them before."

2. Seek to forgive. We cannot honor our parents without first forgiving them, without releasing them from the debt we believe they owe us. Bethany grew up in a home where lies prevailed. "I've learned that honoring means forgiving and releasing my parents of any expectations," she says. "All I can do is pray for them and leave the rest to God—an act I do continually, as my father continues to do hurtful things. I've had to realize that my parents don't always know how to love, and I have to be okay with that."

3. Laugh at sad predictability. This piggybacks on Bethany's insights. She realized her parents didn't always know how to love, and she came to terms with the reality of their behavior. The next step, then, is to incorporate sad predictability into our lives. Instead of letting a parent worry us, we reach the point, as Bethany did, where we realize our parents may never change.

Make a game out of predicting your parents' behavior. Forecast their responses beforehand. Deal with the grief before the responses happen. Then, when they respond just as you thought they would, laugh to yourself instead of being bitter. You won the game!

4. Seek a heavenly view. There are so many more relationships on earth besides our familial ones. Our true family is made up of those who embrace the mission of Jesus. So seek a heavenly view of family. In heaven we all will be children of God under the headship of Christ. We will have eternity with our parents if they become children of God on this side of forever. If they are not his children, we need to pray earnestly on their behalf, model humility and grace before them, and share the good news of Jesus with them as the Holy Spirit prods. And that's all we can do. Our investment in their lives may be limited because of dysfunction or misunderstandings, but in heaven all relationships among those who make it there will be healed.

5. Know the difference between honor and respect. Honor and respect are subtly different. Jack, whose mother slapped and neglected him and modeled immoral behavior, understands the difference. "Mom will always have a place in our life. Honor is not dependent on godly living. However, I had to come to a place where I understood the difference between honor and respect. Respect is earned, or in the case of my mom, it has not been earned. Once I saw the difference, it freed me to honor my mom regardless of who she is."

6. *Let go of guilt.* Honoring our parents means relinquishing the crushing burden of guilt that comes with believing that it's our job to save them. I used to feel that for my mom to be saved, I had to be a perfect Christian. When I failed, I would plunge into deep sadness, thinking, *My mom will never come to Christ now that I've messed up!* I'm weary of these thoughts. When my stepfather called me after years of absence, it was a wonderful reminder that a loved one can be saved through the Holy Spirit's action and presence, without my involvement. I realized how self-centered I was to think it was up to me to save my family. That's the job of the Holy Spirit.

7. *Temper your words.* As I mentioned earlier, we must speak the truth to honor our parents. Truth, though, is not a sharp instrument used to impale others. Instead, we temper our words, seasoning them with grace. Suzanne said, "I try not to slam my parents anymore, but I am still honest. To honor them is not to say only what they want to hear, but to speak truth with grace and mercy and kindness."

8. *Set boundaries.* Grace has to set boundaries with her father—a man who abandoned his family and continues to jab Grace with mean, insensitive words. "When he crosses the line I draw, I tell him. If he is talking ugly about people, I ask him to stop. If he insists that I have too many children or I should not be a missionary, then I tell him he does not have to be a part of our lives. I tell him with real love and no venom in my voice, actions, or attitude. So far, he has accepted this. I believe it is because I genuinely love him, and he senses that."

Entire books have been written about boundaries (see the recommended reading list at the end of this book). In order to protect our hearts and the hearts of our children, the most honoring thing we can do is draw a line and not allow our parents to cross it. Because we love our parents and long to honor them, we want to see them whole and acting righteously. Drawing a boundary says, "I care enough about you and your character that I won't allow you to act a certain way when you're around my family. I want to see you be your best. Therefore, I will not allow this behavior."

9. *Prepare for enjoyment.* "Honor yer Ma and Pa" is the first commandment directed to humans as social beings. The first four commandments deal with our

vertical relationship with God; the last six address our horizontal relationships with others. The apostle Paul pointed out that the "honor" commandment has a promise attached to it: "That it may go well with you and that you may enjoy long life on the earth" (Ephesians 6:3). Learning to honor our parents is a task God rewards—with enjoyment and a long, full life. The greater our degree of honor, the greater our degree of enjoyment. No longer held in bondage by our bitterness or anger, we find that honor frees us to love our parents while we follow our heavenly Parent down new paths.

Give yourself a gift: Start honoring your parents today.

Part II

God Is with You Today

So do not fear, for I am with you;
do not be dismayed, for I am your God.
I will strengthen you and help you;
I will uphold you with my righteous right hand.
—ISAIAH 41:10

If you are like me, you go through your parenting day uttering one-word prayers, such as "Help!" Pioneer parents are bewildered by the dizzying array of parenting books, most of which are not written with our life experiences in view. Couple that with the insecurity that results from our family backgrounds, and it's easy to understand why raising children is such a difficult task for us. Yet God is present with us. He is right here with us today. He is able to help us when we falter or simply don't know what to do.

"I Just Can't Do This Parenting Thing"

Succeeding When You're Weak

Unless the LORD builds the house, they labor in vain who build it.
—PSALM 127:1, NASB

The goal of pioneer parenting isn't to produce perfect children. It's not to prove to the world that we've overcome the past. Neither is it a testimony to our stellar parental capabilities. Our overarching goal can *only* be to know and love Jesus more deeply. Any other goal leads us into the futility of what Larry Crabb calls the "Law of Linearity."[1] We believe that if we do A, B will surely follow. We work harder and harder to perfect A so that we can enjoy the benefits of B.

Here's an example of how this myth of cause and effect colors our thinking. My husband was interviewing people at a shopping mall for an evangelism assignment. He stopped people and asked them questions ranging from nonchalant (such as "Where do you live?") to bridge questions about their belief in God. One couple really got under his skin. When he asked about child rearing, the woman said, "Oh yeah, we're Christians. Our kids turned out splendidly. We taught them the Word. We did everything right. And God blessed it! Our neighbors, on the other hand, well, they weren't believers. They didn't raise their children right. Now their kids are in jail. Raising children in a Christian home assures that kids will turn out well."

You and I both know this woman bought into a lie. First, if you're reading this book, it's likely you didn't grow up in the fertile soil of a Christian home. This woman's reasoning could be an affront to you. Isn't God big enough to pull anyone out of the depths? Isn't his forgiveness freely available to those of us who know we're sinners?

And consider the deeper issue at work here. This woman's apparent smugness is a barrier to intimacy with Jesus. Her pride in thinking she somehow created perfect children erects a wall between her heart and God's. She doesn't see the sinfulness of her assumption that she can somehow control the slippery outcomes of life.

I'm not judging the woman; I'm just recognizing an attitude that I have had myself. I've had the same log in my own eye, and I still struggle with the weight of the beam. I've had to internalize the truth that only God changes hearts. Only God can bring about life-change in my children.

Does this mean we just stand back and let our children run wild, trusting the outcome to God? No. The Bible includes books of wisdom for us to absorb and teach. The real issue is our attitude. If we sincerely believe that we can change our children, then we are delusional. The only Changer is God—and the only way to parent is from a position of weakness. The apostle Paul promised in 2 Corinthians 4:7 that in our jars-of-clay state, God shows up with his power. Allow this verse to serve as a primary source of encouragement: "But we have this treasure in jars of clay to show that this all-surpassing power is from God and not from us."

Feeling ill equipped to parent our children is actually a great advantage. As mere jars of clay, we lament having no healthy example of parenting to follow. The good news is that our weakness in parenting can be a dance floor for God to showcase his "all-surpassing power." He is the true Parent. He is the *only* perfect Parent.

WE'RE ALL CHILDREN OF SINNING PARENTS

Jesus was raised by imperfect earthly parents, just as we were. But his past was not a hindrance to his mission to love the world one person at a time. Neither should our past hinder us from loving the children God places in our homes. Our effectiveness in parenting, which is simply ministering to the little people God puts in our lives, is directly related to our dependence on the Father. Our weaknesses, then, become the playing fields where God can do his work.

If we rely on our commitment to raise our children well, we will fail. But if we instead rely on the strength of the Holy Spirit, through his power we will succeed. Which brings us to this question: What is success? Raising godly children? Having a home that is free from strife? Being admired by other parents? True success is a pilgrim journey, halting at times but always moving forward into the great recesses of God's love. Our children may choose to reject the faith and values we teach them. Even then, if our goal is to know God's strength and to love him more, then, yes, we can succeed. Perfect parenting is not the goal. Knowing the delight of our heavenly Parent is.

Ruth is a mother who lives this truth. Her ex-husband, a con man, spends the week with their son, Christopher, poisoning his young mind against his mother and peppering him with a litany of lies. On the weekends Ruth does her best to deprogram Christopher, who by now is angry and confused.

"I worry I'll be one of those mothers who bails her child out of juvenile hall," Ruth confides. "I worry he'll turn out just like his father. All I can do is love him, take him to church, and pray."

Although desperately trying to gain full custody of Christopher, she has had to relinquish what little control she had and entrust Christopher to Jesus. In the midst of her anguish, she perseveres. She can live only for the applause of heaven.

LOVE GOD, LOVE OTHERS

Jesus taught his followers about the Great Commandment: Love God and love one another. Our job is not to become perfect parents so we can please God or impress others; it's to love Jesus first and foremost. We are to thank him for showing us mercy. We are to remember our own stories of his reaching into the miry clay of our needy lives and placing our feet on higher ground. We are to consider his mysterious ways. We are to worship him with abandon. If that is our goal—to love Jesus passionately—then loving our children will flow naturally from that.

But how does this work in real life? If you're a person who prefers order, a set sequence, and clear formulas, this particular commandment is messy. "Love God; love others" seems too nebulous and idealistic. But that's just on the outside. When you peel away the layers, you find that the Great Commandment is immensely practical and as real today. In a sense, it is God's way of bringing order to our world.

Growing up in a chaotic environment in which I often felt unsafe, I redefined my world by following lists. Lists made me feel as if I had control over a life that sometimes spun on a wild axis. When I put my faith in Christ, I substituted new lists for the old ones. Instead of "Brush your teeth every day," my list now included "Read your Bible every day." Like many survivors of difficult backgrounds, I felt okay when all my plates were spinning happily and none of them fell. Somehow, if I did all the right things, my plates would stay aloft and I would feel safe, in control. Life never allows plates to spin forever, though. Even if I could accomplish everything on my self-assigned lists (which I couldn't), the plates would eventually come crashing down. Life is like that.

When that happened, I'd panic. Suddenly the world I had carefully controlled through my devotion to lists became unsafe and uncharted. I'd cry out to God, ask him why he "did this to me," and wonder where I had gone wrong. Notice all the first-person pronouns in the last few sentences. So much of my life on that Pharisaical treadmill was about me—my ability to live the Christian life, my pride when I succeeded, and my depression when I failed. I wasn't loving God because of his beauty; I loved him out of obligation, because "love God" appeared at the top of my list of good things to do.

When I became a mom, I still kept lists, only this time I replaced some of the old items with a few parenting-specific items, such as "Spare the rod, spoil the child"; "First-time obedience is essential"; and "Let them know who's in charge." Instead of parenting from my weakness—loving God passionately and allowing his strength to help me through chaotic days—I'd make it my goal to be the best mom possible. I based my system of child rearing not on my deep love for Jesus but on my rebellion against my own upbringing.

Parenting became a series of things I should and shouldn't do, a pressure-cooker way to live. I'd picture my children as adults sitting across from a counselor and saying things like, "Yeah, I had an okay childhood, except that my mom did insensitive things. Now I'm scarred for life." At night I'd sit in bed recounting all my mistakes, the things I should have said and all I should have left unsaid.

Often the list of bad-parenting antics outweighed the good, and I'd despair. I'd picture the Proverbs 31 woman shaking her head and scolding me.

It was just about that time when I realized there is no magic formula for perfect parenting, just as there is no magic dieting program.

Setting the Wrong Goals

My parenting goals were all wrong. Sure, it is worthy to want to raise healthy, well-adjusted children who love Jesus. But the means to get there was tripping me up. I thought it was all up to Patrick and me. Like a Pharisee flaunting his phylacteries in public, I'd revel in my children's accomplishments—almost *parading* their accomplishments. Why? Because it validated my parenthood. Such deep parental insecurities rested in my heart that I needed my children to be "perfect" to show that I had been successfully healed from the past.

I'm not the only parent who has struggled with this. Just read one of the family Christmas letters that arrive in your mailbox every December.

> Heather is first chair in the community symphony—the youngest ever to
> hold that position. She has to sit on a phone book to see the conductor!
> Jonathan won first prize in the school science fair, then he went to state
> and won again. A large pharmaceutical company contacted him afterward,
> wanting his formula—they think he's found a cure for Hodgkin's lym-
> phoma. Danielle is the valedictorian of her class and got scholarship offers
> from Harvard, Yale, and Princeton. Please pray for her as she is having a
> hard time deciding. Rory competed in nationals in kite building. His box
> kite won first place. God has really blessed our family this year.

I'm not dismissing these letters. They are entertaining, after all. But I wonder—how many parents' hearts sink when they read about all these perfect children? And among the parents who send letters like that, how many think they were responsible for such amazing children? How many of them are desperately seeking proof that they are okay parents?

How refreshing (and shocking) it would be to read a Christmas letter like this:

Cynthia's been struggling this year in school. She's flunked every class but art. We've tried different medications to get her to focus—some make her hyper, others make her sullen, and all stunt her growth. She throws things at us when she's mad. Meanwhile, Brad got his girlfriend pregnant and has no intention of marrying her. Sylvia quit school and is working at McDonald's. She hopes to make it to fry chef someday. In the midst of it all, God is good, and we endeavor to love him well.

How refreshing! The second letter hints at God's grace in the midst of pain— a message I hope to convey to others and within my family as I love God and love people. The truth is, we can *never* do enough to ensure that someone else will obey God. While God desires for us to follow him, he gave us all free will. He has chosen to let each of us decide whether to put our trust in him. The same holds true for our children: They are free to follow God or reject him.

Parenting in our weakness, then, becomes an exercise in unswerving trust. Will we trust God when our children stray from what we hold dear? Will we love him first and passionately pursue him whether our children delight us or vex us? Will we honor him when we feel like yelling at our children—or at him? Thankfully, God offers our children grace when they fail. He offers us grace when we fail. Our weakness actually opens our eyes to his astounding grace.

God Requires Our Hearts

I have a friend whose father made her sit down after dinner every night to read the Bible aloud. So rigid were his expectations and so harsh was his criticism when she didn't live up to his standards that she eventually rebelled. She struggles now to connect with a God who seems distant, arbitrary, and angry—all because an inflexible father portrayed God as a cruel deity.

What does God require? He requires our hearts. Our affections. Our brokenness. Our allegiance. Our devotion. He wants us to abandon our agendas and embrace his. He wants us to fall in love with him. More important than being a parent, I am a child of the living God. Before I can parent effectively, I must first fall in love with my heavenly Parent.

The Importance of Brokenness

Successful parenting is more about a broken heart that is dependent upon the Mender of all hearts. It's about authenticity and candor with God and with our children. The most life-changing book I've read is *The Calvary Road* by Roy Hession. In it, he speaks about revival. When I first picked up the book, I was a wide-eyed college student longing for revival. I'd picture the students at my campus falling on their knees before God, weeping and repenting. I wanted to know the secret of revival. According to Hession, the secret is brokenness—the epitome of personal weakness:

> It is so often self who tries the Christian life (the mere fact that we use the word "try" indicates that it is self who has the responsibility). It is self, too, who is often doing Christian work. It is always self who gets irritable and envious and resentful and critical and worried. It is self who is hard and unyielding in its attitudes to others. It is self who is shy and self-conscious and reserved. No wonder we need breaking. As long as self is in control, God can do little with us.[2]

If we'd like to see our homes revived by the rushing wind of the Holy Spirit, we must examine what is in our hearts that wants to control life—that part of our hearts that *must* try so hard to do everything just right. A broken heart yielded to Christ produces much fruit. So much of today's parenting literature has to do with strength, resolve. But according to the Sermon on the Mount, it's the weak and feeble who inherit the Kingdom of God. Could it be that we do our children a disservice when we demonstrate how strong and capable we are as parents?

Perhaps your testimony, like mine, cries out against that kind of thinking. When God chose me, I was on the brink of suicide. When he lifted my head from beneath the evergreen tree, I was lost, alone, and quite broken. When he walked me through my past, I was a blubbering mess. As I type these words today, I am keenly aware of my frailty. I assault myself with such thoughts as, *Who do you think you are trying to write a book about parenting? You yell at your children. Sometimes you ignore them. What kind of expert are you?*

My only answer is that I rest on God's grace. Of course I'm not a perfect parent. A perfect parent doesn't exist—unless his name is heavenly Father. I make mistakes. I disappoint my children. Truth be told, I fail at parenting daily.

What keeps me going is *not* my capability; it's my weakness. God's promise to me is that he will be my strength:

> But he said to me, "My grace is sufficient for you, for my power is made perfect in weakness." Therefore I will boast all the more gladly about my weaknesses, so that Christ's power may rest on me. That is why, for Christ's sake, I delight in weaknesses, in insults, in hardships, in persecutions, in difficulties. For when I am weak, then I am strong. (2 Corinthians 12:9-10)

Can you catch the beauty of what Paul was saying in this passage? He has given pioneer parents the incredibly good news that we can *boast* that we had no healthy examples of parenting to learn from as we grew up. We can *delight* in our lack of expertise. Only when we are in that utterly humble place can we know God's amazing strength. Only then can we love God deeply and offer our children holy glimpses of his love. Guilt over our weakness dissolves in the loving embrace of the God who loves to strengthen the weak. Oswald Chambers exhorted, "Every element of self-reliance must be slain by the power of God. Complete weakness and dependence will always be the occasion for the Spirit of God to manifest his power."[3]

When our prayer changes from "Make me a better, more capable parent" to "Lord, help me love you and know your strength when I am weak," we have the privilege of seeing our goal realized.

I have a friend who is an excellent mother. Her adopted daughter, a crack baby, has incredible mood swings. She has tested every limit her mother has set, often with a flippant attitude. She's been disrespectful. She's screamed at her mother. She seems to have no remorse over hurting others. On one occasion when my friend was having a particularly hard day, I asked how I could pray for her. She openly acknowledged her weakness and her inability to know *what* to do. She said, "Pray that I will spend the day in heart and action the way God would have me spend it." Her desire was to first please God, to ask for his strength, to honor him. She knew she couldn't parent her daughter well. She knew she needed Jesus.

"Great," you might say. "So I'm supposed to ask God for his strength when I'm weak? That's all fine and good, but I need *answers*. I need to know how to fix the problems in my life and in my family."

If we are seeking God only for answers and solutions, we are aiming far too low. God is not a holy room-service attendant whom we can order around. He is the Creator of the universe—of the myriad stars that pock the night sky, of the rolling waves of the ocean, of the intricacies of the human heart. Our first allegiance should be to him—no strings attached.

How Little We Know; How Much We Need God

Sometimes answers to our questions never come. Job experienced this when he argued with God and lost. "Surely I spoke of things I did not understand, things too wonderful for me to know" (Job 42:3). Who are *we* to think we can know everything? The Bible says we can't even know our own hearts. We are not placed on this earth to know how to do things successfully or to know all the answers; we are placed here to love the One who created us—even if our children end up rebelling, even if our parents never come to Christ, even if we "fail" as parents.

The one constant in our lives does not come from understanding life's perplexities; it comes from knowing the One who is the Answer to all questions. We cannot, in our own strength, hope to make our children love God and follow him. But we can rest our heads upon the chest of the God who loves our children infinitely more than we do. We can rely on his profound wisdom, his insight, his direction. It's only in that humble position—where we say, "He is God and I am not"—that we experience his grace and power.

"Why Not Just Give Me Some Rules and Be Done with It?"

Pioneer Parenting from the Inside Out

What you're after is truth from the inside out.
Enter me, then; conceive a new, true life.
—Psalm 51:6, MSG

Picture yourself as deli meat. Or peanut butter and jelly, if you prefer. As a pioneer parent, you are part of a unique sandwich, surrounded by bread. Your parents need Jesus. Your children need Jesus. You, as the center, need Jesus. God has strategically placed you where you are, not just for the sake of those in your own generation, but also for the previous generation and the generation that will follow. Instead of seeing your position as frustrating, see it as an amazing opportunity for Kingdom work. You have the potential, through the work of the Holy Spirit, to affect not just one generation of Christians but three: bread, deli meat, bread. What an amazing privilege! What a dizzying honor!

When Patrick and I were first married, we prayed for our extended families. We both believed that God had told us, "Your families will be won to me through the next generation." We are already seeing this happen. Our children are less inhibited. They don't have the history we do with their grandparents. Our son,

Aidan, can get away with a spontaneous "Will you go to heaven?" which has more of an impact on his grandparents than if I asked the same question. One slice of bread is ministering to the other slice.

Consider this: Jesus said, "From everyone who has been given much, much will be demanded; and from the one who has been entrusted with much, much more will be asked" (Luke 12:48). God has entrusted to you a difficult past. He longs for you to learn from it, to be healed of it, and to influence the generations he has placed around you. Instead of viewing your sandwich predicament as a burden, view it as a privilege.

What is your responsibility, then? It is to live an authentic life that invites both your children *and* your parents to experience the wonder of God. It is to lay foundations of stability, honesty, and hope. All this comes about by parenting from the inside out. You must first let God into every area of your heart, even the areas where you have stiff-armed him. Authentic life-change begins first in your heart.

As a pioneer parent, I struggle with confidence. I am constantly afraid that I am doing things to hurt my children. But instead of running to Jesus and pouring out my inadequacies before him, I shudder. I worry. I fret.

I long to be a confident parent whose heart matches my facade of capability. But where does confidence come from? From the Parent of all parents. He gives confidence from the inside. This confidence is based not on the certainty that our children will turn out perfectly but on the understanding that we have daily, hourly access to the God who sympathizes with our weaknesses.

> For we do not have a high priest who is unable to sympathize with our
> weaknesses, but we have one who has been tempted in every way, just as
> we are—yet was without sin. Let us then approach the throne of grace
> with confidence, so that we may receive mercy and find grace to help us
> in our time of need. (Hebrews 4:15-16)

God's grace is available to pioneer parents who are riddled with fear and failure. He renews our insides, which results in a rejuvenation of our parenting. He breathes new life into our parenting.

A CALL TO DIE

And yet, in the midst of the Holy Spirit's dynamic renewal, we are called to die. If we are to be Jesus to our children, we will follow in his steps; and his steps lead to Golgotha, the place of crucifixion. Jesus poured out his life for us. He served others. He became obedient to death on a cross. As parents who long for our children to get amazing glimpses of Jesus through us, we must not shun the path of death. The apostle Paul spoke of death in terms of how his dying to sin and the world benefited those he ministered to:

> We always carry around in our body the death of Jesus, so that the life of Jesus may also be revealed in our body. For we who are alive are always being given over to death for Jesus' sake, so that his life may be revealed in our mortal body. *So then, death is at work in us, but life is at work in you.* (2 Corinthians 4:10-12)

Our death, our walking the path of Golgotha, brings life to our children—specifically, the life of Jesus Christ.

Getting married is one of the methods God uses to refine us, to teach us how to die to our selfish desires. In marriage we are forced to look at our own agendas, to see how self-absorbed we are. We have to consider our partners as more important than ourselves. We have to compromise. We have to take the backseat.

If marriage is a microcosm of the school of discipleship, parenting is God's playing field, wide and open for all to see. As parents, we are called to die to our own comfort, to a good night's sleep, to personal ambitions. Parenting is a crucible, a place where God refines us further, where we, if we bend to his urgings, will embody discipleship.

Yet sometimes we equate discipleship with an "All you have to do is…" mentality. Church leaders have presented Christianity as a series of steps from lesser commitments to higher ones. Instead of being told, "God is asking everything of you," we hear bits and pieces of this grand commitment:

- All you have to do is…pray this prayer.
- All you have to do is…read your Bible every day.

- All you have to do is…raise your children in the church.
- All you have to do is…tithe.

As leaders raise the bar, ordinary Christians become confused. Instead of presenting Christianity first as a call to die, we prescribe it in a series of ever-more-difficult steps. We miss the wisdom of Dietrich Bonhoeffer, who maintained that if we consider Christianity a series of antiseptic steps, "discipleship is no longer discipleship, but a program of our own to be arranged to suit ourselves, and to be judged in accordance with the standards of a rational ethic."[1]

Christ's call to us as believers, as spouses, as parents is a call to death. "As we embark upon discipleship we surrender ourselves to Christ in union with his death—we give over our lives to death. Thus it begins; the cross is not the terrible end to an otherwise God-fearing and happy life, but it meets us at the beginning of our communion with Christ. When Christ calls a man, he bids him come and die."[2]

Before we can establish a parenting-skills tool kit, we must first search our hearts and see if we are who we're supposed to be—believers sold out to God's highest agenda, delightfully resigned to dying to our own agendas and, instead, embracing God's plan for us.

If it is true that children learn primarily by example, then the best parenting method is to learn the art of shedding "All you have to do is…" Christianity so we can embrace the cross as a divine demonstration of true parenting. If we hope for children who will lay down their lives for Christ, we must provide the model, since what we are on the inside is what we ultimately produce in our children.

WHAT PARENTING FROM THE INSIDE OUT LOOKS LIKE

Adhering to methods and formulas is a safe way to assure ourselves that, in spite of our insecurity, we are doing a good job. "See?" we say. "I can grow my children Jesus' way. I've discovered my children's love languages. I know their learning styles. I'm doing fine."

But Jesus contrasted methods and measurement with his inside-out truth when he rebuked the religious leaders for appearing devout on the outside yet having darkened hearts (see Matthew 15:3,6-9). Parenting from the inside out has more to do with the state of our hearts before a holy God than it does with what parenting methods we adopt. Real life-change is never easy to measure. It's gauged by our walking the path with Jesus day by day, step by step, and grace by grace. Parenting from the inside out is not neat and sequential. It is meandering and unpredictable. But it is a transforming tool in the hand of our Savior, which he uses to make us into disciples.

Still, there are some characteristics that define parenting from the inside out. They're not entirely measurable, but they do indicate a shift in how you parent your children.

1. *Being the right tree.* Jesus said, "Every good tree bears good fruit, but a bad tree bears bad fruit" (Matthew 7:17). Christ followers who have put their trust in Jesus' sacrifice on the cross are good trees. The old nature (or bad tree) has now been replaced by a new nature (or good tree). If you worry whether your tree is bearing good fruit, remember this truth: The Holy Spirit of God resides within you and empowers you to parent.

Jesus is the Living Water, ever available to irrigate our thirsty roots (see Psalm 1:3). If we follow him closely, our parenting will prosper, and the good tree that is our life will produce good fruit.

2. *Putting prayer at the center.* Prayer is the most important thing we can do. Diane understood this. She grew up in a home where she felt abandoned—and sometimes had no food to eat. As a parent, she worried that she'd raise her children in the same kind of chaotic home she'd experienced as a child. Yet she prayed faithfully, and today her children love Jesus—something that amazes her. "The best thing I did in parenting them was to pray. I made a lot of mistakes, but I prayed."

Our intimate connection to the Father—the part of us that is hidden and in need of his touch—is what invigorates us to love our children well. Prayer is the conduit to that connection. I confess that there are days when I am prayerless. I'll end the day with a sigh, recounting all the occasions I failed. Last night was such a night. In the quiet of my bed, I reviewed my failures for the day and worried: *When Aidan cried over his report card—because of one B—I should have embraced him, reassured him. When Sophie wanted me to read one more chapter, I should have slowed down enough to oblige her. When Julia wanted to have a water fight, I should have put everything else down and frolicked with her.* Had I been in a more intentional state of prayer, my regrets would have been replaced with the joy that comes from obedience. I may not have done all the things with my children that I should have done, but I would have consciously entrusted my minute-by-minute agenda to God, and he would have heightened my awareness of my children's needs. I also would have felt his presence and delight throughout the day. I am simply a better, more centered parent when I pray.

3. *Putting a stop to "campaign parenting."* When I have failed to run to Jesus to be renewed from the inside out, I've been guilty of "campaign parenting." I'll see an evil such as clean clothes that were dropped down the laundry chute, and I'll gather the children together for a lecture. "This has got to stop," I say. "There shall be no more clean pants and shirts tossed down the laundry chute. If you've worn something once and it's not stained, fold it and put it away. If there are clean clothes dotting your floor, put them away. The washing machine is *only* for dirty clothes. I'm tired of washing, drying, and folding already clean clothes."

They assent, but in a few weeks, when my energy to maintain my campaign is gone, clean pants and shirts once again start appearing in the laundry chute. Campaign parenting—an attempt to influence children with lectures, rules, and angst—seldom works, especially since it depends entirely upon the energy and tenacity of the one initiating the campaign.

The only way I can skirt this problem is by enlisting shared responsibility. If my children can own the problem, if they internalize the clean-clothes-down-the-laundry-chute angst, then my campaign might just succeed. Outside-in parenting, in which I am the outside influence telling my children to do something (and all the responsibility rests upon me), may work for a season. But if I can change it to an inside-out approach in which the children take personal ownership of a task or rule, I will see lasting change.

For instance, I've been known to nag my children about clean rooms. All mothers, I believe, have gone to school for this. I used to say things to my kids like, "You can't go out to play until you clean your room" or "I think there are things multiplying and growing under your bed" or "If you don't clean your room, I'll…[insert your dire consequence of choice here]."

Then one glorious day, my children caught the *Trading Spaces* bug. I'd rented a few episodes of this television show where neighbors swap houses and redecorate an entire room, which either shocks or delights the other family. My children were hooked. They traded rooms with one another. With joy and vigor, they cleaned one another's rooms and rearranged furniture, displayed knickknacks in interesting ways, put away toys, and reveled in their decorating prowess. When the time came for the "reveal," each child jumped and screamed. Somehow my children internalized room cleaning, and as they did, they cleaned *one another's* rooms with joy.

LESSONS FROM JESUS

In the Sermon on the Mount, Jesus spoke of hidden things, of overlooked traits. Consider his words, beautifully rendered in *The Message:*

- "You're blessed when you're at the end of your rope. With less of you there is more of God and his rule" (Matthew 5:3). When we break on the inside, there's more room for God to shine through our cracks, for his light to spill over into our children's hearts.
- "You're blessed when you feel you've lost what is most dear to you. Only then can you be embraced by the One most dear to you" (verse 4). Parenthood is a constant letting go. There are times our children drift, unleashing grief in our hearts. That grief, if given to the Grief Bearer, will be redeemed. When we grieve, we have the surprising joy of feeling his embrace.
- "You're blessed when you're content with just who you are—no more, no less. That's the moment you find yourselves proud owners of everything that can't be bought" (verse 5). Contentment with who we are is an inside-out endeavor. We'll be blessed when we are truly content with the outside, when we understand God's beauty on the inside. What a gift that is.
- "You're blessed when you've worked up a good appetite for God. He's food and drink in the best meal you'll ever eat" (verse 6). Our appetites are an inner craving. As pioneer parents, we must work up a good appetite for the only One who can fill us. We, perhaps more than most, need the reassuring presence of a joyful heavenly Parent.
- "You're blessed when you care. At the moment of being 'care-full,' you find yourselves cared for" (verse 7). Often, caring for children and family

is a task that's invisible to others. Even when the needs of others overwhelm us, even when our care is unseen, God cares for us. He will restore our hearts.

- "You're blessed when you get your inside world—your mind and heart—put right. Then you can see God in the outside world" (verse 8). The core of parenting from the inside out is letting God into our inner worlds. With that part settled before God, he will help us navigate our outside worlds, where children and spouses and extended family await us.

- "You're blessed when you can show people how to cooperate instead of compete or fight. That's when you discover who you really are, and your place in God's family" (verse 9). A perfect verse for parents of toddlers, or any children! Cooperation is often caught, not taught. How often I've seen my children bicker the way I bicker or raise their voices with the same lilt and intonation I use. To teach cooperation, I must experience a God-sized Copernican revolution in my heart, so I can become a peacemaker from the inside out.

So What?

Why should we take an inward look? Why should we allow God to examine our hearts? Because true change happens when our hearts change. Because purposeful parenting proceeds from healed hearts. Because when we choose to disavow our inner neediness and wear an all-is-well mask, we don't change the past, we lose the future.

Remember, you're deli meat. God has positioned you strategically between two generations. Let him transform you from the inside out so that you can be an agent of transformation for your parents' generation, your children's generation, and the generations that will follow.

"Even When They're Whining—or I Am?"

Parenting with Gratitude

Be joyful always; pray continually; give thanks in all circumstances,
for this is God's will for you in Christ Jesus.
—1 THESSALONIANS 5:16-18

I'm an Eeyore. I have the spiritual gift of being able to determine the worst possible scenario for any given situation. I'd like to call myself a realist, but the truth is that I'm a pessimist. I expect bad things to happen. I worry even when I *escape* expected dire circumstances. Instead of being thankful for the beauty of one sunshiny day, I stew about possible rain tomorrow. Instead of being thankful that my twelve-year-old daughter brought home good grades, I fret about her becoming a teenager.

Even with such a bent toward negativity, I grew up singing—so much so that my mother scolded me for singing at the dinner table. The songs I gravitated toward most were those written with minor chords. Songs like "One Tin Soldier" resonated with me; the melancholy melody connected with my Eeyore heart. The odd thing about minor chords is that they are disguised major chords with a flat central note. Perhaps I gravitated toward minor-key songs as a child because, at the center of my life, I was flat, out of sync.

3. He rests in and trusts in God's power and goodness. I've had a hard time believing in God's power and goodness. Because God seemed powerless to help me when I was five and boys sexually molested me, I've wondered about his capabilities. Because he didn't protect me from harm, I've wrestled with his goodness. But I am determined to exercise gratitude nonetheless. I've made David's declaration my own: "I am still confident of this: I will see the goodness of the LORD in the land of the living" (Psalm 27:13). Even when current circumstances whirl out of control, I long to be grateful, to thank God for his power, for his goodness. How can I possibly do this? By waiting. David gave himself wise advice in verse 14: "Wait for the LORD; be strong and take heart and wait for the LORD."

4. She is aware of God's grace moment by moment. A gratitude-based parent recognizes that *everything* that constitutes her life—finances, children, health, relationships—is based on God's grace, not on her own merit. The more we understand God's grace, the more we will live grateful lives and see gratitude spill over into our children's lives. James the apostle said, "Don't be deceived, my dear brothers. Every good and perfect gift is from above, coming down from the Father of the heavenly lights" (James 1:16-17).

Any gift or talent we've received, any skill in parenting comes from God's gracious hand. "For who makes you different from anyone else?" Paul asked. "What do you have that you did not receive?" (1 Corinthians 4:7). Because God bestows on us grace upon grace, we can bestow it to our children.

5. He knows that God's nearness equals his good. Nothing of eternal significance is wrought without God's intervention. God's nearness, or our nearness to God, helps us parent. Like a weaker ox yoked to a powerhouse ox, we benefit from the strength of the Powerful One. If we understand our need for him, we'll begin to see changes in our parenting.

6. She doesn't play the comparison game. Perfect Christian parents seem to be everywhere, and their "error-free" lives mock our fledgling attempts at pioneer parenthood. If we play the comparison game, always measuring ourselves against other parents, we'll cease to be thankful. The truth is, there are no perfect parents. I've spent too much of my life envying others' apparent parenting successes. But I will not be free to exude gratitude unless I take my eyes off others—and myself—and fix them solely on the only Perfect Parent.

From Minor to Major Key

What if the parenting metaphor were a song? Our Perfect Parent is a musician who sings over us. One of the Old Testament prophets assures us,

The LORD your God is with you,
  he is mighty to save.
He will take great delight in you,
  he will quiet you with his love,
  he will rejoice over you with singing. (Zephaniah 3:17)

We sing with and over our children, hoping the melody of heaven will awaken their hearts. Together, our families create songs—songs of joy, disappointment, elation, fatigue. I've sung scores of melancholy songs that awakened bitterness and resentment in my heart. I long to sing in the major key, to proclaim God's goodness in the midst of my parenting. After all, "It is easier to sing your worries away than to reason them away."[1]

In the Scriptures, singing and gratitude are inexorably linked:

Let them sacrifice thank offerings
  and tell of his works with songs of joy. (Psalm 107:22)

Let the word of Christ dwell in you richly as you teach and admonish one
another with all wisdom, and as you sing psalms, hymns and spiritual
songs with gratitude in your hearts to God. (Colossians 3:16)

As pioneer parents, we'd do well to sing through our days, lifting both our dirges and our declarations of praise to the Father, who sings over us and enables us to parent with gratitude and grace.

11

"But I'm Not a Handyman!"

A New Way to Build Your Family

> *I have not failed. I've just found ten*
> *thousand ways that don't work.*
> —THOMAS EDISON

King Solomon built the temple in ancient Jerusalem—a magnificent structure meant to honor and revere God. He built God's "home" and yet his personal life did not show God the honor and reverence due him. That's the fear of my life—that in building things that appear to honor God, I could end up sacrificing my personal integrity and thus failing as a parent.

It's interesting that Solomon penned these words: "Unless the LORD builds the house, its builders labor in vain. Unless the LORD watches over the city, the watchmen stand guard in vain" (Psalm 127:1). To build a house, a place where a family reveres and honors God, we must rely on God's labor and protection.

We are co-laborers with God in this impossible task of rearing our children. He is their ultimate Parent; we are but shadows of his grace. And yet, as we are yoked to the Lord, we build our family. Still, as pioneer parents, we have no blueprint to work from. Because of our upbringings, we look at our old blueprints in confusion. We know which doorways are too low. We know we don't want the same leaky roof. But we don't know which modifications to make. We don't even have the proper tools.

We vow to emulate a passage such as Deuteronomy 6:6-9:

> These commandments that I give you today are to be upon your hearts.
> Impress them on your children. Talk about them when you sit at home
> and when you walk along the road, when you lie down and when you get
> up. Tie them as symbols on your hands and bind them on your foreheads.
> Write them on the doorframes of your houses and on your gates.

The problem is, we don't have a healthy doorframe on which to hang the commandments.

THE NEW BLUEPRINT

Pioneer parents have to find new ways to build a family. We need to build from new blueprints—blueprints the Lord creates afresh. Following is a family blueprint that reflects God's desires for our families.

A Family of Love

The foundation for our families must be love. Without it, according to the apostle Paul, our parenting is nothing more than "a resounding gong or a clanging cymbal" (1 Corinthians 13:1). We may be the best engager of our children's imaginations and the greatest helper with homework, but if we lack love, we lack everything. Dr. Ross Campbell, in his book *How to Really Love Your Child,* says, "Only this foundation of unconditional love can assure prevention of such problems as feelings of resentment, being unloved, guilt, fear, insecurity."[1]

Paul put an exclamation point on the importance of love. He listed several amazing attributes we should strive for and then elevated love above them all:

> Therefore, as God's chosen people, holy and dearly loved, clothe yourselves
> with compassion, kindness, humility, gentleness and patience. Bear with
> each other and forgive whatever grievances you may have against one

another. Forgive as the Lord forgave you. And over all these virtues put on love, *which binds them all together in perfect unity.* (Colossians 3:12-14)

Love is a binding force. It infuses and holds all other virtues together. Love is the preeminent trait we should embody as parents. Campbell writes:

"Almost every study I know indicates that every child wants to know of his parents, 'do you love me?' A child asks this emotional question mostly in his behavior, seldom verbally. The answer to this question is absolutely the most important thing in any child's life."[2]

I remember asking that question often when I was growing up because I didn't feel loved. My fear today, as I've mentioned before, is that my children will feel the same way.

How do we build a foundation of love? The only answer is *a relationship with Love himself.* God is love. If we know him, we will know love. John the apostle wrote, "Dear friends, since God so loved us, we also ought to love one another. No one has ever seen God; but if we love one another, God lives in us and his love is made complete in us" (1 John 4:11-12). God's love is made complete in us when we grasp his love for us, and that love is then translated to our children. In loving God and others, we are perfected in love.

Love can't be engineered, though. I don't wake up and say, "Okay. I am determined to love my children." It flows directly from my love relationship with Jesus. Oswald Chambers wrote, "The springs of love are in God, not in us. It is absurd to look for the love of God in our hearts naturally, it is only there when it has been shed abroad in our hearts by the Holy Spirit."[3] The best gift I can give my children is to fall in love with Jesus. The more I know of him—his forgiveness, his peace, his joy, his grace, and his ways—the more his love flows through me to my children.

Sophie, our eldest daughter, struggled with our family's move to France to plant a church. Before we left the states, we stood side by side in church while we sang a worship song titled "Your Renown." The words speak of living for God's renown, for his glory. As I prayed and sang those words of love to Jesus, I noticed Sophie's heaving chest and cradled her shoulders as we sang. I experienced the majesty and love of Jesus in that song, and that experience made me want to love and embrace my grieving daughter. Love begets love.

A Family of Prayer

If love is the foundation of our home, prayer is its support beam. Without it, we are powerless to love. Prayer is our intimate connection with an empowering, grace-filled, holy God—a God who delights to strengthen us.

It's simple enough to say but difficult to practice: Prayer must be modeled if we are to establish a family of prayer. Our children run to God when they see us run to God. They see God's faithfulness when a family prayer is answered. One tangible thing we've done in our home is to hang a chalkboard in our dining room. We call it our prayer board. Throughout the week we write down the date and a prayer request and then leave a space for an answer. This simple tool reminds us to pray for more than our meals. It also serves as an encouragement. The children see God answering prayer as they record his faithfulness on the chalkboard.

Prayer is a powerful weapon in defeating Satan's destructive plans for our children. When my son, Aidan, has a discouraging day at school, he sometimes plunges into "I'm no good. I'm a horrible person." That's when I stop and pray for him on the spot. I don't want him believing Satan's lie that he has no worth.

Prayer soothes wounded children. When my daughter Julia is afraid of monsters in her closet, she asks us to pray. When we do, she calms down and goes to sleep.

A Family of Storytelling

Storytelling adds depth, beauty, and aesthetics to any family. Gladys Hunt, in her groundbreaking book *Honey for a Child's Heart,* expounds the virtues of stories:

> Take all the words available in the human vocabulary and read them from
> the dictionary, and you have only a list of words. But with the creativity
> and imagination God has given human beings, let these words flow
> together in the right order and they give wings to the spirit.[4]

To create a home of stories, we read. When we read, our children catch the value of reading. When we read to them, we recapture their hearts and attention. What a joy it has been to read stories to my children, meeting for the first time people like Laura Ingalls, Anne with an *e,* Christy, Frodo, Alec, and so many more. There is no trading the closeness that reading brings to a family. Even if we sat on the couch under blankets, eating popcorn and watching a movie, we couldn't engage the hearts and minds of our children as much as if we read to them.

The added bonus is that parents and children interact with the stories. They place themselves within the stories. They observe when capricious characters get in trouble. They watch an oppressed character demonstrate mercy even when revenge seemed in order. They realize that the world is unfair and that God is bigger than the world and is able to weave redemption even through the darkest of circumstances. A shared vocabulary develops when we speak with our children about the stories we've read and how they parallel or apply to life.

In preparation for leaving for France as church planters, I decided to read Randy Alcorn's *Safely Home* to my two older children. I wanted them to understand persecution because I knew we'd face opposition while we served as missionaries. My children not only learned about the underground church in China, but they understood that living for Jesus in other parts of the world can mean severe persecution. A redemptive story prepared their hearts for a difficult move.

A Family of Scripture Reading

Scripture is the framework of a home. We need to live, breathe, memorize, and practice the Word of God. That means telling the great stories of the Bible, familiarizing our children with the central doctrines of the Christian faith, and actively teaching others.[5] The Word of God is our greatest parenting textbook. In it we read these words from Proverbs 22:

> Train a child in the way he should go,
>   and when he is old he will not turn from it. (verse 6)

> Folly is bound up in the heart of a child,
>   but the rod of discipline will drive it far from him. (verse 15)

When I have lacked wisdom in parenting, I've found the Proverbs to be a great tool. Read a portion of Proverbs every day, for wisdom's sake, but be sure to read it with a humble heart. It's easier to find the folly in our children on the pages of Proverbs than it is to see our own propensity for sin and foolishness. Read it as if God were speaking directly to you.

The Word of God will only be inviting and exciting to our children if we live it. I knew a girl whose father used the Bible like a hammer. When she disobeyed, he bludgeoned her with platitudes from its pages. He did not pause to let the words transform him, producing the fruit of patience, joy, perseverance, and gentleness. Instead, he pointed the finger at his daughter's disobedience. The apostle James said, "Do not merely listen to the word, and so deceive yourselves. Do what it says" (James 1:22). It's easy to show others where they are falling short; it's a far greater thing to listen to God's words and actually obey them.

In your zeal to teach the Scriptures to your children, be sure you aren't missing the life of Jesus (see John 5:39-40). His Spirit is what gives us life. He illuminates the Word of God to our children. He pours out strength and joy and patience into our own hearts. In your zeal for words, beware that you don't forget the Word of Life.

A Family of Laughter

If Scripture is the framework of our home, laughter is its electrical outlets, giving energy and vitality to every room. Laughter is what makes life bearable. It breaks tension. It releases endorphins. It sets us free from taking life too seriously. William Makepeace Thackeray captured the essence of a laughing home when he said, "A good laugh is sunshine in a house."[6] We instill laughter by using a hefty dose of don't-take-life-too-seriously. Let go of the frown and laugh with your children. This is such an important part of family life, particularly for pioneer parents, that we'll return to the necessity of humor in a later chapter.

A Family of Listening

Listening is the intercom system of our family. So often, I'm quick to jump on my children instead of listening to them. James wrote, "Everyone should be quick to listen, slow to speak and slow to become angry" (James 1:19). As a pioneer parent, I often revert to how I was raised. If I don't take time to listen, I'll say words I'll regret later, the same words that stung *me* as a child.

An overlooked aspect of listening is the practice of listening to the Lord. If I long to be a parent who breaks from her past, I must listen to the Lord—the

Author of redemption. People have asked me, "Why do you say you've heard God? I never hear God." Part of my response has been, "Because I've walked a long way with him, and I've learned to listen." Like author Jack Deere, I've learned the life-changing lesson that I need to place my confidence in his voice, not in my ears. "Humble people put their confidence in the Holy Spirit's ability to speak, not in their ability to hear," Deere writes, "and Christ's ability to lead, not in their ability to follow."[7]

A Family of Celebration

Celebration is our family's playroom. Patrick and I create a celebratory home using a little ingenuity and organization. Our family celebrates every birthday by throwing an original party, taking pictures, and creating interesting cakes and surprising party favors. During Aidan's Thomas the Tank Engine phase, I made a Thomas cake. The frosting dyed our hands and mouths blue! For Julia, our flower child, I made a daisy cake, with edible-flower cupcake tops. Since Sophie's birthday falls on Christmas Eve, we celebrate her half birthday on June 24, complete with a swimming party. Although our celebrations aren't expensive or elaborate, we have a terrific time playing relaxed games and enjoying the company of our children's friends.

In addition, Patrick and I trade planning our anniversary celebrations. We make heart-shaped desserts on Valentine's Day. We think about Saint Patrick on March 17 by listening to a Focus on the Family tape about the life of Saint Patrick and talking about his missionary life. We anonymously give flowers to our neighbors on May Day.

We take our kids out to dinner on report-card days. We gather with friends on Thanksgiving, rejoicing in God's provision. We endeavor to have meaningful, less materialistic Christmases. Last year, we opted to make all our Christmas gifts. This helped our kids focus more on the joy of giving than on what they would receive. So they were more gracious when they received a handmade gift from a sibling.

Celebrating traditions, however small or grand, brings balance and rhythm to a family. It provides a framework for the year. It gives children the chance to anticipate, participate, and relish a family gathering. Unfortunately, we've packed our lives so full of tradition-less activities that we've lost the art of anticipation. We rush through the moment, robbing ourselves of celebration.

A Family of Feasting

Feasting is the family's dining room, the heart and soul of its structure. It's tragic that regularly sharing meals together has become passé, a relic from the nation's farming past. It takes planning to have a home of feasting. To make it happen, you need to be proactive:

- Turn off the television during mealtimes, and eat around your table. Sharing time together over a meal enables you to focus on one another. Minimizing distractions will do more for your family dynamic than any other family ritual.
- Try to keep dinnertime at the same time, and guard that time as the most sacred appointment on your calendar.
- Involve your children in making dinner. This helps when you get to the food-pushing stage. If they've helped chop the veggies, perhaps they will eat them! (Note the word *perhaps*—there are no guarantees!) Also, have the entire family help with cleanup.
- Keep the conversation going, encouraging each family member to share what happened during the day. Try not to discuss heavy adult issues. The table should be a lighthearted place where children and adults know they are listened to, valued, and cheered.
- Don't answer the phone. This is part of keeping your family time sacred.
- Keep it simple. Easy recipes, rendered by loving hands, are enough. Dig out that wedding present Crock-Pot and have at it.

A Family of Recreation and Relaxation

Many of us live in homes of hurry-up-and-get-to-the-next-event. The minivan has replaced the home as the place where we live, eat, and interact. We forget that the four walls of our homes are meant to shelter our families from a chaotic world. A house of recreation and relaxation is built with hefty doses of margin. Dr. Richard Swenson defines margin as "the amount allowed beyond that which is needed. It is something held in reserve for contingencies or unanticipated situations. Margin is the gap between rest and exhaustion, the space between breathing freely and suffocating. It is the leeway we once had between ourselves and our limits."[8]

We have become a culture of "indoorsmen," huddled around a television, eat-

ing fast food, and darting outside just long enough to run here and there in fre-
netic activity. Mary Pipher believes that "many modern children find it safer and
easier to stay indoors and watch television. I worry that children do not even
know what they are missing. In the wilderness there is connection and complex-
ity, challenge and serenity. In most of us there is a deep hunger for contact with
the natural world."[9]

We need to make space in our families and in our lives for downtime, for
recreation, for getting outdoors, for nature, for giggling, for unstructured play. If
we long to embrace and educate our children in God's ways, we must spend time
with them. As I mentioned earlier, values are caught, not taught. In order for our
children to catch our values—much like one catches a cold—they must spend a
lot of time around us. If we fail to spend significant time together, our values will
seem distant, unimportant. Family time becomes reality only when we build margin into our lives.

A Family of Training

Training is what makes our families move and exist within a Christian worldview.
Many of the Scriptures referring to child rearing deal with the concept of training. You must be deliberate in training your children, no matter what form it
takes: reading the Bible, praying together, sharing Jesus with others, living a
lifestyle of mercy toward those less fortunate. The difficulty in this area for pioneer parents is the comparison game. We watch other parents train their children
well and suddenly feel as if we are failures for not doing it the same way.

A third-generation Christian parent might continue a practice modeled from
her childhood by memorizing verses of Scripture with her children every night at
bedtime. She may teach her children to use a prayer journal. But such practices
might seem to you as foreign as speaking French. So as you train your children,
it's important that you don't berate yourself for not "looking" like other parents.
Sharing Jesus with your children may be as simple as watching the stars together,
reveling in his creation. It may take the form of simple prayers at bedtime for a
lost pet or for an unsaved friend. It may be as intangible as being there for your
child, attending his games or recitals.

The best way to learn how to train our children is to ask Jesus what he wants
for them. Our way of training may look entirely different from that of other

parents. The key is that we are seeking God and spending authentic, intentional time with our children. In training them with dedication, we must verbalize our plans, be utterly consistent, and discipline with a heart of grace.

Training is really discipleship. Think how Jesus discipled his twelve closest followers. He walked dusty roads with them. They shared meals. They fished. They served. They rested. They prayed. That's the model for discipleship we need to implement in our families—a day-to-day connection with our children that manifests the life of Jesus in every circumstance.

A Family of Encouragement

To encourage simply means "to give courage to." Without encouragement, our children will feel disconnected. They will not view home as a haven. Eventually, they'll listen to other "encouraging" voices instead of ours. As pioneer parents, we may have grown up without encouragement. Instead of genuine praise, we received stinging criticism or, worse, indifference.

Encouragement is the language of love. If we fail to speak it into the hearts and emotions of our children, they will forget we love them. No matter how you were raised, it is imperative that you learn the art of encouragement. If you're at a loss, consider using some of these encouraging words:

- I like the way you folded the laundry today.
- I know you really studied hard for that test. Great job!
- When you hugged your sister, I saw God's tenderness in you.
- Thank you for the card. Your words mean so much to me.

Be sure your words have more to do with what's happening inside your child than with her performance. Praise her character, her burgeoning relationship with Jesus, her kindness, her ability to be empathetic. Instead of stroking a child's ego, encourage the heart. In praising these character qualities, you reaffirm the truth that "the LORD does not look at the things man looks at. Man looks at the outward appearance, but the LORD looks at the heart" (1 Samuel 16:7).

A Family of Jesus Followers

To build a family of Jesus followers, we use the tool of lifestyle, patterning our lives after the One who died for us. That means reading *and* living out the Sermon on the Mount—the longest sermon Jesus gave. Our children need to see this

sermon lived and breathed in our homes. One of the turning points in my relationship with Jesus came when I realized that his words in this sermon weren't just
beautiful words to etch on plaques or emblazon on T-shirts; they were meant to
be *obeyed*.

Consider my paraphrase of portions of Matthew 5–7:

Have mercy. Be pure. Be a peacemaker. Rejoice when you are persecuted.

Be salt and light to a tasteless and dark world. Don't call other people
names or think murderous thoughts.

Settle things quickly. Don't allow grudges to fester. Don't lust after
what isn't yours.

Shun divorce.

Let your yes be simply yes—be authentic in your speech. Turn the
cheek to the one who accosts. Walk two miles with a stranger who asks
you to walk one.

Give to anyone. Love your enemies. Pray for the persecutor. Do good
in secret. Pray in secret. Forgive others.

Think in terms of your heavenly bank account. Don't love money.
Don't worry. Trust the God who cares about sparrows and flowers.

Use discernment, not harsh judgment. Ask things of God. Believe he
answers and longs to give you good gifts.

Produce fruit. Know Jesus.

Reread the paraphrase, this time thinking in terms of your family. Do you
forgive one another? Are you quick to judge? Do you truly believe and demonstrate to your children that God answers prayer? Do you say what you mean and
mean what you say? Do you know Jesus?

The soul of our families is our ability to follow in Jesus' steps, to live as he
did. Our children will know more about him as we emulate his words than if we
preached a hundred sermons.

A Family of Healthy Fear

As pioneer parents, we may have grown up with a keen sense of fear. But the house
where fear reigns is a crumbling house.

Instead, our houses must be protected by the fear of God. We must be sheltered by a healthy reverence for the One who created heaven, flies, grass, toes, hearts, spider webs, sunshine, a viable earth. The tool we use to erect this roof over our families is everyday reverence.

Reverence means "to hold God in high regard." It's understanding that he is completely different from you, including the uncomfortable fact that God is holy and you are not. It's not that you shrink back in fear, worrying that he's in the sky carrying a stick to hit you when you fail. No, it's understanding the beauty and miracle of his love, that he, being holy, dared to stoop to the earth and offer his Son as a sacrifice for your unholy life. With that as a backdrop, you can live your life in hushed awe because the perfect God made a way for imperfect you to know him.

Perhaps the reason so many children turn from God in their teen years is that they've never been taught to revere God. Rather than being stunned by God's greatness and his grace, they are dismissive of him. Consider Proverbs 14:26: "He who fears the LORD has a secure fortress, and for his children it will be a refuge." Fearing God brings security to our homes—a refuge for our children. And Jeremiah 32:39: "I will give them singleness of heart and action, so that they will always fear me for their own good and the good of their children after them." Our fear of God brings good to our children *and* our grandchildren. As pioneer parents wanting to initiate a godly heritage, we should find great encouragement in this.

A Family of Grace

I started this family-building analogy with love, and I'll end it with grace. We infuse our homes with grace through our transparency. Our children need to know that we fail. When we do fail, they need to see us run afresh into the arms of Jesus. We want to model the prodigal son's father—ever welcoming, ever extending grace—so our children will have an accurate picture of the Lord as they leave our homes and go out into a graceless world.

WISE AND FOOLISH BUILDERS

Solomon was the wisest man of his time. He built a temple for the Lord, and yet he was a fool, forsaking God in ways small and large. Still, he understood that only the Lord could build a house. Hopefully, we'll be wise enough to realize that we can't build our homes by ourselves. We need Jesus, the divine Carpenter, to build our homes. As pioneer parents, we need his scarred hands to draw the blueprints for our families and build in the characteristics presented in this chapter. Only then can our homes and families withstand the onslaught of this world.

Jesus said,

> Therefore everyone who hears these words of mine and puts them into practice is like a wise man who built his house on the rock. The rain came down, the streams rose, and the winds blew and beat against that house; yet it did not fall, because it had its foundation on the rock. But everyone who hears these words of mine and does not put them into practice is like a foolish man who built his house on sand. The rain came down, the streams rose, and the winds blew and beat against that house, and it fell with a great crash. (Matthew 7:24-27)

Building our families upon the foundation of Jesus Christ is our primary strategy.

12

"Oops, We Did It Again"

Forgiving Yourself; Forgiving Your Children

*Children seldom misquote you. In fact, they usually
repeat word for word what you shouldn't have said.*
—UNKNOWN

Every one of us lives in a houseful of sinners. From big people to small, we step on each other's egos, saying words that inflate rather than deflate an argument. We all disobey God, causing chaos.

No home is immune from this. My son, Aidan, didn't need to be taught how to pit one parent against the other. It came naturally. So when he pulled it again, asking me if he could do something when his daddy had already said no, I asked him why he did it.

"I accidentally did it on purpose," he cried.

We have a lot of "accidentally did it on purpose" in our house. The fact is, because of human nature, we all enjoy sinning. Even though we've been made completely new in Christ, our tendency is to fall back on what is easy, what we think will satisfy. When each family member lives with a me-first attitude, the need for repentance and forgiveness intensifies.

Parents have a powerful influence over their children. How we model Jesus Christ is how our children will view him. If we never admit our own flaws and sin, if we blame our children for our own outbursts, they will view God as I often have, as an angry drill sergeant in the sky. If we want our children to understand the grace-filled God who stands with his eyes fixed on the horizon waiting for his prodigals to come home, we must extend grace to our children and ourselves.

The way we practically work that out is through forgiveness. It is inevitable that we will make mistakes. We will fail. We will say and do things we wish we hadn't—things we can't erase. But God will forgive us. He will take away the shame, guilt, and personal disappointment. He will wash us clean, make us new. We need to extend that same grace to ourselves—forgiving ourselves for our propensity to accidentally do things on purpose. Just as important as asking God for forgiveness and extending it to ourselves is learning to forgive our children for their disobedience. To model grace, we must be forgivers.

FORGIVE YOURSELF

Many of us have a lopsided view of forgiveness: We see it as something we do for other people. However, a radical understanding of God's forgiveness not only frees us to love others; it also enables us to forgive ourselves, to extend grace to our own needy hearts.

Starting with God's Forgiveness

Forgiving ourselves is based solely on the amazing forgiveness Jesus demonstrated and secured on the cross. Taking our sin upon himself, he felt the wrath of a holy God burn into his being so that we wouldn't *ever* have to experience that holy wrath. While humanity hurled insults at the Lamb of God, he extended forgiveness. Because of Jesus' radical act of obedience on the cross and his victory over death, we can approach God the Father using words like *Abba,* which means Daddy. Jesus made a way for us to sit on the lap of our heavenly Daddy.

Often, though, when we speak of forgiveness, we speak in terms of other people rather than ourselves. "I forgive her for those unkind words," we say. But what if we say unkind words to our children? Often our response is, "I should have known better. When will I ever get it right? I'm a horrible parent." Yes, we are all unworthy. But in our unworthiness, Jesus dared to die for us. The problem is that we freely extend forgiveness to others and neglect extending it to ourselves. We forget that we are his children, too, and in desperate need of his grace.

Confessing Our Sins to Our Children

Part of the reason we don't forgive ourselves is that we don't model repentance in front of our children. We don't admit our sin to them. Repentance is a communal activity. If we don't speak of our failures in front of others and ask for forgiveness, our self-doubt will berate us in the secret places of our hearts. The less we say aloud, the more our hearts receive messages of condemnation. God has called us to walk in the light, to admit our sin in community. Read the following verses carefully. I've used a nontraditional translation in hopes that the fresh wording will surprise you. The reference appears at the end.

We saw it, we heard it, and now we're telling you so you can experience it along with us, this experience of communion with the Father and his Son, Jesus Christ. Our motive for writing is simply this: We want you to enjoy this, too.

The writer sets the stage by inviting us to experience joy—explaining that if we experience communion with the Father and his Son, we will have this joy.

Your joy will double our joy!
        This, in essence, is the message we heard from Christ and are passing on to you: God is light, pure light; there's not a trace of darkness in him.
        If we claim that we experience a shared life with him and continue to stumble around in the dark, we're obviously lying through our teeth—we're not living what we claim.

Notice how the writer uses the word *we,* meaning that if we stumble in our sin, we do so in community. Yet if we choose to allow God's light to penetrate our sin, to allow him to spotlight it before our children, we'll be purged, forgiven within the context of community.

But if we walk in the light, God himself being the light, we also experience *a shared life with one another,* as the sacrificed blood of Jesus, God's Son, purges all our sin.

If we claim that we're free of sin, we're only fooling ourselves. A claim like that is errant nonsense.

Again, the author is speaking of community, using the phraseology "a shared life with one another." Walking in the light involves community. If we deny our sin, particularly in front of our children, we are fooling ourselves.

On the other hand, if we admit our sins—make a clean breast of them— he won't let us down; he'll be true to himself. He'll forgive our sins and purge us of all wrongdoing. (1 John 1:3-9, MSG)

That's the famed verse some of us memorized when we first met Jesus. Yet we wrongly claim the verse as an "I" verse. *If I confess my sins, he is faithful and just to forgive my sins.* Confession happens in community, as does forgiveness. Some believe that letting our children see our sins and weaknesses will erode our parental power, and our children will disrespect us if we appear weak. This is based on a parenting model of intimidation, not relationship.

Be careful that you don't fall back on such a flawed model. Pioneer parenting is based on relationship. Yes, authority must be acknowledged in the home, but to consider it the most important trait of parenting is to invite rebellion. Confessing our sins to our children does not undermine our authority; it endears us to our children. It invites our children to offer us forgiveness, a skill they'll need to learn and practice the rest of their lives. It frees our children from worrying that they are always wrong and we are always right. It gives children an authentic picture of the grace-filled Parent that our God is. It helps them understand grace and offer it to others.

Confessing our sins to our children benefits us as well. There is something amazing that happens when my daughter wraps her arms around my neck, kisses my cheek, and says, "That's okay, mommy; we all make mistakes. I forgive you." Suddenly it's easier to forgive myself because my children extend such grace.

Letting Go of Regret

Inevitably we carry some amount of parental regret. Freedom from regret comes when we admit our weaknesses before Jesus. No one is perfect. Our imperfections, though, shouldn't become a wall between God and us or our children and God.

At the cross we can lay down our regrets over our failures and move on. Remember that even the great heroes of the Bible did things they regretted. Moses, David, and Paul each wrote a big chunk of the Bible, and they were *murderers*. Still, God used them mightily. Like David, all we can do is ask God to forgive us and then move on. Likewise, Paul knew he was far from perfect. Consider his words as you wrestle with regret:

Not that I have already obtained all this, or have already been made perfect, but I press on to take hold of that for which Christ Jesus took hold of me. Brothers, I do not consider myself yet to have taken hold of it. But one thing I do: Forgetting what is behind and straining toward what is ahead, I press on toward the goal to win the prize for which God has called me heavenward in Christ Jesus. (Philippians 3:12-14)

What a revolution there would be in our homes if we *lived* these verses! We live in a microcosm of sinners who bother and perplex one another. Yet at times we expect our children to be perfect. No one has attained perfect holiness, and this side of heaven no one will. And still, Paul set an example for us to keep going. Yes, we may have regrets. Yes, we may wound. But we serve a bleeding Savior who died to secure forgiveness for our sins. We are forgiven—of past sins, of present sins, of sins yet to be committed. With Paul, we must strain toward what is ahead. Regret will cause us to stagnate—possibly by falling back into the patterns of our upbringing. Regret is just one more thing we must give to Jesus, letting his capable hands wash it away.

FORGIVE YOUR CHILDREN

Our children will not understand forgiveness if we don't model it. If we act as constant critics, our children will grow up feeling unloved and unworthy. No child is perfect. No child will meet our every expectation. Like us, they fail. Like us, they need grace. It's time to acknowledge that and learn to model forgiveness.

Starting with God's Forgiveness

We are able to forgive because God has already forgiven us. If you struggle with forgiving a rebellious, smart-alecky, or wayward child, remember this: Your tower of sin is much bigger. Consider your entire life. Pile the sins atop one another and see how they tower toward the moon, swaying this way and that. Jesus has forgiven your every sin, every level of the tower. In fact, as you stand before God the Father, you have no tower, because Jesus adorned himself with your tower of sin on the cross. Amazing grace, indeed!

Now consider the sins your children have committed against you. Even if you added them all together, they would amount to nothing more than a small tower. Because God forgave our colossal tower of sins, should we not forgive the smaller towers of sin our children commit? Their sin directed toward us doesn't compare to *all our sin* directed toward a holy God.

Following a New Blueprint

The blueprint of your home is being redrawn. A house of forgiveness is attainable if you model repentance. Your children, then, will know how to tell the truth and repent of their own sins. Without their repentance, the road to forgiveness is nebulous and convoluted.

It's heartening to see my children repent in the same manner Patrick and I do. They are learning perhaps the most valuable lesson of life: that to say "I'm sorry" is the primary language of Christianity. The new blueprint is one that will be passed on for generations.

Basing Forgiveness on Truth

Our children must first tell the truth about their sin in the context of the family community to be able to experience the beauty of forgiveness. Don't settle for half repentance. Forgiveness should be given freely in a home, but only when the truth has been shared.

Julia, our youngest, broke one of Aidan's pottery projects, but she wouldn't admit it. She blamed her friend. She stomped her feet and, with tears, said, "I did not do it." Several days later, Patrick and I asked again about the broken pottery. And as before, Julia denied it. Eventually, we asked her again, "Did you break the pottery?"

A single tear became a river. Her little body racked with sobs, she said, "Yes, I did it." It was only then we could extend forgiveness to her because she had finally acknowledged her sin. Two months later, when Julia came home from school one day, she spent an hour playing and then approached me, head down. Tears became rivers. "Mommy, I got in trouble at school today," she admitted. Without my having to press her, she confessed how she got in trouble. Had Patrick and I not kept pressing her about the pottery incident, I doubt she would have come to us about getting in trouble at school. Forgiveness is a costly act and must be accompanied by truth; otherwise it is not truly forgiveness.

We do our children harm if we gloss over their sin. We do even more harm if we don't press truth telling. How sad it's been to watch parents believe their children's lies, which enables the children to continue misbehaving. For example, when a girl named Ellie visited her friend Nancy, she broke Nancy's sister's bike. Ellie had been the only person riding the bike when it broke, yet she said she didn't break it. Her parents believed her. She learned that it paid to lie—that when telling the truth would get her in trouble, it's better to lie. For children to truly understand and experience forgiveness, they must first be taught that truth telling is supremely important.

Assuming a Positive Intent

This will seem like a contradiction of the previous point, but it is not. As in all aspects of life, parenting is a journey of paradoxes. We must press for truth, but we must do so with kind intention. Instead of jumping to conclusions when we think our children have disobeyed, we must hold back, pray, and not always assume the worst.

When our son, Aidan, was two years old, he bit his eldest sister—a lot. One day Sophie came running to me, crying. She said, "Maybe Aidan was nervous and thought I was pie."

Sophie assumed positive intent. She believed Aidan's bites were an indication of his love for pie rather than a malicious desire to harm her. Likewise, when our children act up, it's important to first take a deep breath and pray, asking Jesus for his insight. Instead of assuming the worst, ask questions. When Julia screams, "Aidan is trying to kill me," I can smile, say a prayer, and ask Aidan what he was trying to do. Not always, but often enough, what I had assumed didn't quite match the facts. If we place a high value on truth in our homes and are committed to assuming positive intent, we will enable our children to tell the truth. They know they will be heard. They know their parents won't jump to conclusions—that we'll listen to their side before rendering a decision.

Forgiving with Grace

When Sophie was five and Aidan was maddeningly two, he liked to come into her room and knock over her china tea set, sending it crashing to the carpet. Then, of course, he'd smile. One day after such an incident, Sophie cried, wiped her tears, and told me, "I love Aidan even when he comes in my room and sins."

In the family, all of us upset one another's tea sets. We might even do so with a smile. All of us would do well to utter the grace-infused words, "I love you even when you come into my life and sin." Our love for our children isn't connected to their behavior, just as God's love for us isn't connected to our behavior. The only reliable connector between our children and ourselves is grace, just as grace is the primary quality that keeps us nestled against the Father. Undeserved grace. Grace based on God's surprising love, not our incapacitating sin. As we forgive our children, we embody and demonstrate holy grace.

ACCIDENTALLY ON PURPOSE

We all sin "accidentally on purpose." No home is immune. The binding force that holds your family together is the generous offering of forgiveness. As pioneer parents, we may not have experienced forgiveness in our homes while growing up. Nonetheless, we can experience it today as we forgive our children and ourselves.

We are most like Jesus when we forgive, and we will experience him more as we embrace that holy occupation within our homes. After all, it is his forgiveness that enabled us to embrace him in the first place.

"But What If I Messed Up?"

Using Your Past Sins to Teach Your Kids

As far as the east is from the west,
so far has he removed our transgressions from us.
—PSALM 103:12

Scars from a painful childhood can cause us to make poor choices during adolescence. And poor choices can create paralyzing regret, which can stifle our parenting when our children reach the adolescent years. We don't want to appear to be guilty of hypocrisy, so we may cower from saying to our children, "Don't do drugs" if we took drugs, or "Don't have premarital sex" if we had premarital sex.

But does our own history *really* disqualify us from encouraging our children to walk a pure path? Truth be told, we're all hypocrites. The only perfect human—the only Person not plagued by hypocrisy—was Jesus. His followers were hypocrites, including a former cowardly liar and a former murderer who wrote most of the New Testament. Our sin does not disqualify us from teaching God's values and commands to others.

Consider your own regret over certain past choices. Knowing the lingering remorse created by unwise life choices, wouldn't you want to do everything in your power to help your children avoid the same mistakes? Who better than a parent who still feels the sting of regret to help guide children in wise paths?

Flawed parents are fully qualified to guide their children in righteous living.

But our response to our sin *can* prevent us from providing the direction our children need. Moses, David, and Paul recognized their sin and repented. They all trekked through years of exile prior to or following their sin. In that exile, God taught them many things, including how to live for him in light of past violence. God taught them dependence, and eventually they emerged from exile, teaching others the wisdom and fear of God. It's the same pattern for us. We must acknowledge our sin before a holy God and turn away from it. We must walk through years of exiled healing when God teaches us how to live for him and for others. Then, with God's strength, we must teach what we've learned to our children.

The place to begin is forgiveness. Before we can move past regret, we must know we are utterly forgiven. Every sin we've committed has been paid for by Jesus Christ. He loved us enough to place himself on the cross and pay the price we never could have paid. Because of Christ, hypocrites like you and me are clean, spotless.

My Struggle

I struggled for several years with an addiction to sexually explicit romance novels. Because I kept it a secret, I lived with nearly debilitating shame and guilt. I grew up in an environment of sixties "free love." Although I never saw people have sex, I was accustomed to seeing naked grownups, particularly at my father's house. It was part of the culture—free, naked, unencumbered. That ignited my curiosity about sex. When I found books in our home library that had detailed descriptions of the act, I couldn't seem to stop reading them.

As I've looked back at that struggle and God's wonderful deliverance in my early twenties, I see clearly how my environment led to my addiction to explicit novels. At age five, I learned that a woman's body was to be used for the gratification of men or boys. In my father's home, I saw the lines between decency and luridness blur. I was exposed to the darker sides of sex, which were imprinted on my mind and prepared me for the books I would devour later.

Even so, I take responsibility for my sin. Regardless of my upbringing, I chose to let these books strangle my mind and darken my view of sex. But Jesus Christ set me free, whispered words of grace in my ears, and cleansed my mind. I am deeply ashamed of what I read and the way it poisoned my mind, just as I am deeply astounded at how Jesus conquered my sin when he offered the only perfect sacrifice on the cross.

Someday, as each of my children reaches an appropriate age and the situation warrants it, I will tell them of my struggles with this form of pornography. It won't be easy, but as the Lord opens the door, I hope I will be brave enough to walk through it, modeling redemption, authenticity, and humility. With pornography so readily available on the Internet, and considering the devastation it leaves in its path, why would I not do everything I can to steer my children away from it?

Even though we've failed in our battle with sin, we can still point our children to the One who never sinned. We can say, "Don't do as I did, but do as God says" because, as redeemed sinners, we understand his strength.

EXAMINING THE EXCUSES

Finding the strength to honestly tell our children *not* to do what we did is not easy. We use many excuses, some legitimate, some not. Let's consider the most common excuses.

"I'm Embarrassed"

I *am* embarrassed. A girl who read books with blatant sex scenes? For years I felt that if my secret ever got out, I'd be disqualified to be a Christian. The embarrassment was so great, I couldn't even write my struggles out for fear that writing them would heap more guilt upon me. Then I found freedom in the Light. When I hid my sin, Satan had a wily way of heaping piles of rubbish on my heart. The darkness that inhabited my mind was so great that I thought God must hate me. Even Scripture seemed to confirm that I was no longer the Lord's: "No one who is born of God will continue to sin, because God's seed remains in him; he cannot go on sinning, because he has been born of God" (1 John 3:9). As long as I remained in hiding, not sharing my sin with others, the Enemy kept his heavy cloak of shame and guilt and wrath over me.

Even worse was my false perception that the sexual relationship was dirty. I did not have God's perspective on sex—two people becoming one as a holy union.

Perhaps because I experienced the dirtiness of sex as a small child, the books I read strongly confirmed to me that sex was vulgar.

Then I found my release in 1 John 1:7: "But if we walk in the light, as he is in the light, we have fellowship with one another, and the blood of Jesus, his Son, purifies us from all sin." I didn't experience freedom until I longed for God's white-hot holiness more than I fretted about my embarrassment. When I confessed my reading preferences to a few trusted friends, the cloud of wrathful darkness lifted immediately. I was able to walk away from sexually explicit novels. Now I am repulsed by any hint of sexually impure material.

Will I be embarrassed when I tell my children about this part of my story? Of course. Sin is shameful. It is ugly. My sin humiliated Jesus. My sin brought darkness and wrath upon his perfect shoulders. I pray I will share my story in a way that shows the importance of walking in the light. I pray my story will serve as a cautionary tale. As I tell it, I'll marvel at the surprising grace of Jesus—that he still chose me despite my utter failures. It's a message I want my children to hold in their hearts: that they serve a God who waits for them, who welcomes them with open arms, even if they've been wallowing in pig slop.

"The Timing's Not Right"

The matter of timing might prevent us from sharing our stories with our children. This is a legitimate concern. Telling young children of our adolescent escapades is not wise. In this innocence-busting world, one of our parental duties is to insulate and protect our children from the stain of humanity's sin—to protect their innocence. Yet Jesus told his followers, "I am sending you out like sheep among wolves. Therefore be as shrewd as snakes and as innocent as doves" (Matthew 10:16). Eventually our children will reach the age when we'll send them into the world as "sheep among wolves." May our stories be the fodder God uses to teach them shrewdness.

Of course, the Lord may prevent us from sharing at all, or he might tell us to wait. How we share is intimately tied to our close relationship with the Lord. Walking the line between innocence and shrewdness with our children is difficult, and it can only be navigated through prayer. Each circumstance is different. Each child is different. We may find that telling one child our story would be damaging, but it might prove to be redemptive for another. Before we decide whether to share our past sins, we must be in constant communication with the Lord for wisdom and timing. Consider asking others to pray for you. And keep in mind that in some cases the timing is *never* right.

"My Sins Are Worse Than the Sins of Others"

There's an unofficial but influential measuring stick out there, measuring our sins from zero to twelve. It works something like this:

- Adultery, fornication, drunkenness, and murder—all these get a twelve.
- Gossip? Well, not so bad—maybe a three.
- Not showing mercy? A two.
- Neglecting to show hospitality? Maybe a two point five.
- Raising our voices at a slowpoke on the freeway? A one, for sure.

Jesus has nothing to do with this measuring stick. He broke it into pieces, particularly during the Sermon on the Mount when he said that to look lustfully at another person is the same as adultery and that thinking murderous thoughts is the same as the actual deed. True, sins committed against the body have different repercussions. The apostle Paul said,

> Flee from sexual immorality. All other sins a man commits are outside his body, but he who sins sexually sins against his own body. Do you not know that your body is a temple of the Holy Spirit, who is in you, whom you have received from God? You are not your own; you were bought at a price. Therefore honor God with your body. (1 Corinthians 6:18-20)

Even so, sin is sin, whether it is gossip, sexual sin, dishonesty, or drunkenness. All of it is shameful. All of it looks like filth under the holy scrutiny of Christ. All of it needs to be confessed. No matter what your sin, don't allow your man-made measuring stick to prevent you from confessing it.

THE BEST WAYS TO IMPART WISDOM

If you've wrestled through your regrets and have laid them at the foot of the cross, and if, in your communion with Jesus, you feel he's telling you to share your stories with your children, how do you go about it? How do you tell your children to "do as God says" rather than repeat your youthful sins?

Share Cautionary Tales

Pioneer parents reveal our own weaknesses and propensity for sin in order to teach that sin may feel great for a season, but it will end up devouring us. We share our stories as one would read *Grimm's Fairy Tales*—as stories with a moral. "This is what happened to me when I was caught up in that sin."

We can do this even when our children are younger. A good rule of thumb is to relate stories that happened when you were the age your children are now, unless the story involves violence or sexual abuse. Last year I was able to share my most embarrassing fifth-grade moment with my then eleven-year-old daughter. When I told her how I wet my pants on the Scrambler, a carnival ride, and how I got the girl I was with sopping wet, my daughter learned the importance of telling the truth—particularly when you need to go to the bathroom.

Other topics are more serious. Scott chose to share some excruciating news with his son. "I arranged for an abortion for my girlfriend in college," he explains. "I told my son about it when he was graduating from high school. It was tough, but I figured it would also be a good learning experience. Actions have consequences. He needed to hear about my own bad decisions and the pain it caused me and others."

We can share cautionary tales because we've been forgiven. We share because we've learned from our foray into sin. Even David shared cautionary stories *because* he experienced God's salvation. After Nathan the prophet confronted him about his adultery and conspiracy to commit murder, David prayed, "Restore to me the joy of Your salvation and sustain me with a willing spirit" (Psalm 51:12, NASB). Immediately following, he said, "Then I will teach transgressors Your ways, and sinners will be converted to You" (verse 13, NASB). Our experience of God's grace enables us to teach our children his ways.

Share the Sin Law: You Will Be Found Out

As we share our stories with our children, it's important to emphasize the law of sin: "Be sure that your sin will find you out" (Numbers 32:23). Before Christmas

I shared my Rub-a-Dub dolly story with my children. I was a curious third grader who pined for a doll named Rub-a-Dub. My mother warned me, "Don't snoop around for your Christmas presents." Even so, I scoured the house, hoping my parents bought her for me. Sure enough, one day I found Rub-a-Dub smiling at me through a cellophane-encased box in my mom's closet. Problem was, I kept needing to visit poor Rub-a-Dub. Unbeknownst to me, my stepfather had laid a trap for me using string and the hinge of the closet door. I was found out—big time.

Walking through the Proverbs with your children will help awaken your own memories of being found out.[1] Share the following Scriptures, accompanied by a Rub-a-Dub-esque story:

> He who walks in integrity walks securely,
> But he who perverts his ways will be found out. (Proverbs 10:9, NASB)

> Though his hatred covers itself with guile,
> His wickedness will be revealed before the assembly. (Proverbs 26:26, NASB)

Sharing how we were found out will help our children feel safe to share their struggles. Our confession provides a positive atmosphere for our children to be authentic, struggling believers. In addition to sharing the sin law, we can pray that the Lord will help our children confess their sins—and if they don't, that he will provide real-life consequences in answer to their sins.

BROKENNESS IS THE WAY TO GOD'S HEART

Sharing our stories with our children helps set the tone for a home full of authentic, broken Christians. It will be excruciating to divulge our sordid pasts, if God leads us to do so. In that honesty and brokenness, though, our children will see that God calls sinners—not the sinless—to himself. He welcomes the broken, not the fixed. He forgives the offender, not the hider.

King David said this of God:

> You do not delight in sacrifice, or I would bring it;
>   you do not take pleasure in burnt offerings.

The sacrifices of God are a broken spirit;
>   a broken and contrite heart,
>   O God, you will not despise. (Psalm 51:16-17)

God embraces the broken. It's a lesson we need to teach our children.

When I share my struggles with our children, I'll remind them of this verse: "Remember your leaders, who spoke the word of God to you. Consider the outcome of their way of life and imitate their faith. Jesus Christ is the same yesterday and today and forever" (Hebrews 13:7-8).

Patrick and I are the leaders of our home. We speak the Word of God to our children. We hope the outcome of our lives glorifies God. We hope we have a faith worth imitating. Even so, we fail. Yet the author of Hebrews linked the leader verse with a reference to the unchangeableness of Jesus for a reason: People will fail us. We can imitate them all we want, but they will sin. Yet Jesus Christ is the same. He won't fail. His Word endures forever. Even though we've failed, we can say with confidence, "Don't do as I did, but do as God says."

It's important to remember that we are fellow pilgrims on this faith journey with our children. We all stray from God in a hundred different ways. All we can do is admit our failures together and cling to the Changeless One.

"A Funny Thing Happened While Raising My Kids"

Adding the Missing Ingredient—Laughter

What happens if people try to be God? I never tried that.
—JULIA DeMUTH, budding comedian

If you grew up in a dysfunctional home, there is a strong likelihood you had to grow up fast. At an early age I felt like a mini-adult, responsible for parenting my parents. This did not leave much room for childhood, or laughter, for that matter.

Today I worry that I take life far too seriously, and I fear I take that seriousness into my parenting. When Aidan brings home a marked-up spelling test, I come down too hard on him. When Julia spills something, instead of reacting kindly, I raise my voice—as if spilled juice merited it—and berate her for being so, well, kidlike! I lecture. I fume. All because I see life in terms of shades of gray and black. My prayer is that somehow I'd recapture the youth I lost, that I'd begin to give myself permission to scribble with colors like vermilion and magenta. I want to be a pioneer parent who laughs with and at life and who invites my children along for the hilarious ride.

Scientists agree. A recent study revealed that humor or laughing stimulated the same area of the brain as cocaine. According to *Neuron*—yes, this is the name of a real magazine—Stanford University neuroscientists observed sixteen folks who looked at forty-two funny cartoons and forty-two not-funny cartoons. The funny cartoons stimulated the reward system of the brain.[1] The lesson is this: Laughing is better than drugs. Laughing is free. Laughing has no side effects, other than the occasional snort or the wetting of one's pants if things really get out of control.

THE MISSING INGREDIENT

Even if you don't struggle with being too much of a "heavy" in your home, this chapter will provide a welcome relief from most parenting books. Humor can do wonders for your perspective as a parent. Laughter is a powerful way to relieve tension and defuse anger. It helps heal us when we're grieving. Following are some ways we can incorporate humor and laughter into our parenting, even if we have a natural bent toward the serious side.

1. Become like a child. Children loved to scramble onto Jesus' lap. He was irresistible to children. He laughed. He tousled hair and welcomed faith-filled questions. And he instructed adults to become like children—to recapture that carefree innocence they once had. Ever notice how much a child laughs? Just for the sake of experimentation, try to laugh every half hour today and see if it doesn't change your outlook.

2. Be observant. Part of fostering a home filled with laughter is simply being aware of life. If we are too busy or too distracted, we'll miss the many opportunities to lighten up and enjoy our children. Because I am a work in progress, I'm relying on a couple of funny friends to help me flesh out this chapter. My friend Jeanne offers this encouragement:

> My foremost advice to parents would be: Delight in your children and let them know it. When they say something adorable, tell them you think it's adorable. When they stretch their humor muscles, encourage them, whether it's a silly costume they've thrown together or a lame joke they created.

I make sure I laugh when my children say goofy things. I revel in their laughter when I dare to step outside myself and act silly. But I can't do any of these things if I am detached from life, forgetting to observe and immerse myself in it.

3. Remember. Not only do I try to live in the moment with my children and my husband, who is goofy, but I also try to record funny moments. If I didn't, I wouldn't have the following treasury of DeMuth kids' sayings:

- "I don't want to watch Anne with Green Bagels."
- "My thoughts are being controlled by my imaginary friend."
- "I want to be literal. Can I?"
- "Who is better? Satan or a muffin?"
- "When the moon is upside down, it looks like a toenail."
- "There is no life in cereal."

My friend Jeanne also knows the importance of remembering:

Remembering makes me laugh as hard as I did when funny things happened the first time. My daughter Grace graduated third in her class in high school, so she was supposed to give the closing prayer, lead the school song, tell the students to move their tassels, and then toss her cap. She was so worried about tossing the cap correctly, she took hers off right after the prayer and threw it. But instead of tossing it up, she threw it straight ahead like a ninja star. It narrowly missed the photographer's head! He picked it up and gave it back to her. Then she had to lead the school song, and so on, after having done that. I was laughing so hard I thought I'd fall over. I'm laughing now typing it.

4. Laugh at yourself. Learning to laugh at myself is not easy. Often I can laugh in retrospect, particularly if I look back on times when I was a walking stress-o-meter. A case in point is the Great Philadelphia Airport Caper. One thing that endears my husband to me—and one of the reasons I married him—is his unique, dry sense of humor. I love that he is able to laugh at himself and not take life so seriously. While we were waiting for the plane that failed to arrive on time (which would put us home after midnight the night before our children's first day of school), Patrick was able to enjoy the time while I fumed. He held a slice of really greasy pizza in front of me and said, "At least the pizza's good." Parenting with laughter is a learned art!

5. Share laughter. If we can learn to laugh at ourselves, if we can cultivate the childlike attitude Jesus entreated us to incorporate, we then set the stage to share laughter with our children. They realize that laughing is part of a healthy home because we've given them permission to giggle at life. Mark Twain once said, "Against the assault of laughter nothing can stand."[2] Some of my happiest moments with my children involve shared laughter, particularly around the dinner table. It's infectious, creating even more laughter.

6. *Watch funny movies; read funny books.* Sometimes shared laughter doesn't emerge from our circumstances as much as it arises from our shared experiences with media or books. We're a *Princess Bride* family. We enjoy watching funny movies together and quoting the lines. We've read *Amelia Bedelia* and *Mrs. Piggle-Wiggle* together and all burst into giggles. Part of the fun has been remembering those times and repeating funny lines.

7. *Find humor in spite of reality.* Pamela has the best laugh I've ever heard—the kind of laugh that ignites a stodgy theater full of people. When I first met her, I decided she must have had the happiest life of anyone I knew. Not true. For years she and her husband struggled with infertility, yet through it all, she laughed, even amid her tears. One summer Pamela and I sat at a picnic table surrounded by mountains. "I went through my last procedure. It failed," she said. We cried together. But a few moments later, we were laughing. One year later, on the shores of a Canadian lake, we were dedicating their baby boy to the Lord—an adopted miracle.

Pamela still laughs; her laugh is accompanied by a giggle from her son. I love her ability to laugh despite her circumstances; it reminds me of the words, "I have learned to be content whatever the circumstances. I know what it is to be in need, and I know what it is to have plenty. I have learned the secret of being content in any and every situation, whether well fed or hungry, whether living in plenty or in want" (Philippians 4:11-12).

Since I tend toward pessimism, Pamela's example is one I hope to emulate, especially in my parenting. Whether or not my children obey, my hope is that I can still laugh and still be lighthearted and joyful. This ability comes only through my heart's close proximity to the God who created laughter in the first place.

8. *Sing away the blues.* We are a singing home. Sometimes I'll sing rules to the kids. Sometimes I'll recite on-the-spot poetry, eventually setting it to song:

Sophie's room is a big, fat mess.
I have stepped upon her dress.
If she does not clean it now,
Her mommy may just birth a cow.

We watch musicals and wildly weird computer-animated vegetables and belt out tunes at appropriate moments: "My Favorite Things," when a thunderstorm hits, and "The Hairbrush Song," when our children have lost something. Singing, like laughter, breaks tension and lightens the atmosphere. We've cultivated a similar taste in music, so that when we drive down the road in our oh-so-cool station wagon, we can crank up U2 and croon all things Bono.

9. Recount and create embarrassing moments. Our children love to hear about our embarrassing moments. When Patrick recounts his first day of public school—seventh grade, no less—when he was the only boy wearing overalls, our children laugh. Our telling of embarrassing tales helps our children realize that making mistakes and looking foolish are just part of life. The blessing of embarrassing moments is laughing about them later.

We have a friend who specializes in creating embarrassing moments. Once, during a patriotic movie, he stood up in the theater and led the entire audience in a spirited rendition of "The Star-Spangled Banner." Really!

While eating with Sophie one day at school, I teased, "Sophie, what would you do if I stood on this lunch table and sang a song—really loud?" I didn't, of course, but it scared her out of her wits to think I might actually do it. Sometimes, inviting the possibility of embarrassment can bring humor to a boring or monotonous situation. Obviously, it is important to gauge the moment. It is never good to intentionally embarrass a child.

10. Enjoy the health of humor. Instilling laughter in our homes is a prescription for health. King Solomon—the wise man of wise men—extolled the virtues of an upwardly turned mouth:

All the days of the afflicted are bad,
But a cheerful heart has a continual feast.

(Proverbs 15:15, NASB)

A cheerful heart is good medicine,
>   but a crushed spirit dries up the bones.
>   (Proverbs 17:22)

Teaching and living these verses will affect not only our physical well-being but our stress level as well. It's nearly impossible to feel stress when we laugh. Consider the health benefits of humor:

- Humor therapy has become a new way of dealing with stress.
- Jonathan Swift said, "The best doctors in the world are Dr. Diet, Dr. Quiet, and Dr. Merryman." As pioneer parents, we need to visit Dr. Merryman at least three times a day!
- Adults laugh about fifteen times a day—much less than children.
- Laughter releases endorphins. It also reduces muscle tension, stimulates the heart and lungs, and increases the oxygen level in the blood.
- Laughter stimulates the immune system, even activating T cells.[3]
- Bill Cosby said, "If you can laugh at it, you can survive it."

11. Surprise! Spontaneity is an important element of healthy family life. My children know I am a jumpy person by nature, easily startled. So they jump out at me at surprising moments. They love to watch me scream or see my parcels fly helter-skelter. Patrick and I sometimes pretend we're serious when we're not. When our children ask, "What are we going to do today?" we sometimes answer, "Eat lima beans" or "Run around the house in our swimsuits." We try to keep the kids guessing and, when appropriate, surprise them.

12. Don't take yourself too seriously. My mom often gave me the sage advice that it's not good to take yourself too seriously. I still struggle with taking myself too seriously, especially concerning my parenting—which is serious business.

My friend Jeanne learned the surprising truth that laughter bursts forth even during serious parental moments:

Once I was lecturing Luke about something he'd done wrong. I felt like I had to instill a godly perspective in his heathen little head, and I put on my best holy face. I really thought I was getting through to him. He kept staring so intently at my face as I spoke. Then, right in the middle of my speech, he reached up, spread his tiny fingers into a V, and pinched my nose between his index and middle finger! I busted out laughing, lost my train of thought, and said, "Luke! Why'd you pinch my nose?" He laughed too and said he didn't know. I hugged him and left the room. End of lecture. Beginning of camaraderie with my son.

If we long to train our children for life, it's imperative we cultivate laughter. Without it, we may produce pious children but not children who will scramble onto Jesus' lap.

Through a difficult childhood, the painful years of healing, and your current season of parenthood, may you be able to sing—with a smile on your face—"The joy of the LORD is [my] strength" (Nehemiah 8:10). And may that song of laughter become the song of your family.

"Why Can't I Go to Grandpa's House?"

Protecting Your Children While Preserving the Relationship

Daddy, did you know Grandma and her boyfriend have sleepovers?
—DAUGHTER TO FATHER

All of us grew up in homes with flawed parents, and our natural tendencies will be to repeat certain patterns we experienced while growing up. However, as pioneer parents, we desire to establish a new, Jesus-centered pattern in our homes.

I remember coming home from Young Life Camp at age fifteen, when I was a naive new Christian.

"Mom, do you know Jesus?" I asked.

"What?"

"You know. Like if you died today, would you be sure you'd go to heaven?"

My mom tapped her fingers and averted her gaze. She took a breath and said, "Mary, when I die, I'm dead. That's it."

I had always feared my mother, mainly because I had a very real fear that she wouldn't like me if I did anything against her wishes. I found out that day that following Jesus was *not* her wish. And from that day on, I knew that almost every decision I made would not meet with her approval and that tension and disapproval would characterize our relationship. Once I got married, my mom thought

Patrick and I should be concerned about overpopulation and have only one child. After two children, we had tipped the scales, and after three, the ozone layer was sporting a gaping hole, thanks to our progeny.

CHILDREN AND THEIR GRANDPARENTS

When my daughter Sophie was five, we flew across the country to visit our families. For a few days we stayed with my mother and her boyfriend. My mother is an animal lover. Her office is lined with photos and paintings of her current animals and animals that have passed on. One such painting depicted my mother's deceased horse. Sophie saw it and asked, "What is that a picture of, Memaw?"

"My thoroughbred. She's in heaven."

I took a deep breath. Sophie piped up, "No, she's not, Memaw. Horses don't go to heaven. How can they believe in Jesus?"

My mother responded by saying, "My horse is in heaven because she believes in me."

Later during our visit, my mother argued with Sophie when Sophie mentioned God in a masculine way. "Sophie," she said to my five-year-old, "how do you know God is not a woman?"

"Don't be silly, Memaw," my daughter replied. "God's not a woman."

Ever since this exchange, I have been fearful of how exactly to walk the tightrope between protecting our children and letting them stand on their own with their grandparents. Sometimes I totter to one side, allowing grandparents to have too much influence on our children. At other times I fear that I threaten our children's relationships with their grandparents by keeping them apart.

As much as we possibly can, we must preserve the innocence of our children. Unlike God, we can't be everywhere. Still, there are things we *can* do to protect our children from the influence of relatives who may pose a risk.

1. Pray. Since we can't be everywhere our children are, our greatest weapon is prayer. When our children spend time with family members who don't share our values, it is imperative that we pray. God loves our children infinitely more than we do, and he is able to protect them. He is also able to put apt words in their mouths, as was the case when Sophie happily refuted her grandmother's suggestion that God was a woman.

When your children visit difficult relatives, pray that

- God would inhabit the home your children are visiting and that your children would not be tempted to follow after secular philosophies.
- God would put a song in their hearts, a desire to praise him in the midst of relatives who may not follow him.
- your children would be winsome reflections of the love of God.
- God would protect your children from secular media—magazines, books, movies, and television shows.
- your children would make right choices.
- your children would be prayerful and alert during their stay.
- your children would deeply love and enjoy their grandparents and that God would use the visit to bring your parents to himself through the witness of your children.
- God would give your children responses to difficult or probing questions relatives may ask.
- your children would turn to God if or when they are afraid.

2. Overcome fear. I am afraid as I write this. I am worried that my mother will read the advice in this chapter and be deeply offended. I am afraid that someday our children will wander from the faith, perhaps because of the influence of relatives. But if I live in fear, never letting our children experience the joy and wonder of a relationship with their grandparents, I will rob them of a vital life experience. God is bigger than my fears, and he is able to protect our children far better than I can.

3. Ask open-ended questions. After your children visit their grandparents, or an aunt or uncle, ask questions:

- How was your stay?
- What was the best thing about your visit?
- How did you sleep?
- Was there anything that bothered you about the visit?

By asking open-ended questions—in which children are allowed freedom to talk—you invite dialogue. You can explore the visit without interjecting your opinion. Jack asked his four-year-old daughter, Stephanie, open-ended questions after she said, "Daddy, did you know Grandma and her boyfriend have sleepovers?"

"Where did her boyfriend sleep?" Jack asked.

"In Grandma's room, of course!"

"I'm so glad you shared that with us." Before continuing, Jack prayed and then said, "Jesus would like us to have sleepovers only when we're married."

Later he reflected, "I wanted Stephanie to know that we were sad that her Christian Grandma did that, because a sleepover is not what Jesus would want."

When dealing with parents who may *not* be Christians, however, it's important to realize that they are not held to the same standard we as Christians hold for ourselves. If a parent is unmarried but living with someone, and she doesn't yet know Christ, this may not be a valid reason to keep your children away. These are the types of issues we, as pioneer parents, navigate with much prayer. There are certain choices made by non-Christian relatives that *would* prevent us from sending our children over, such as being addicted to crack or having a home full of accessible pornography. But, as in life, there are gray areas. If you are confused as to whether you are judging a relative too harshly, or you worry that you are endangering your children, ask a trusted friend for help. Sometimes someone outside the situation can discern it better.

Even if you decide it's safe enough to send your children to a relative who does things contrary to your beliefs, engage in conversation with your children before and after the visit. Keep asking those open-ended questions, gently helping your children grasp that not all people follow Jesus, that not all make choices that honor him. Reassure them that Jesus loves that relative, and we are to do the same.

4. Communicate openly. Probably the most difficult thing for me to do is communicate my boundaries and expectations with members of my extended family. When I send our children to visit their grandparents, I provide a detailed schedule, try to cover every contingency, provide emergency contacts, tell my family what types of TV programs and movies are appropriate, and try to give them a glimpse into what makes each child tick—one is afraid of dogs, another will push bedtime limits, one cries easily. It is even harder to talk of deeper issues. What if a grandparent favors one child over another? What if there is pornography in your parents' home? What if there are safety issues in the home?

This is where a vital relationship with the Lord comes into play. He will help us communicate the difficult things. I've had to have difficult conversations like this, exchanges that can only be described by the word *excruciating*.

WHEN TO LIMIT VISITS

When God gives us the courage to communicate openly, sharing limits and expectations with our parents, sometimes they don't respond well. They may balk at our expectations. They may continue in habits we deem unsuitable for our children to be around. In these cases, we can't allow our children to be alone with their grandparents. Scott found this to be true. "My mom didn't like one of our children," he says, "so we always had to be there in order to protect that child from her indifference."

In addition to buffering our children, we may have to make the decision to restrict visits or ban them altogether. Jack, whose mother had sleepovers with her boyfriend, said, "Yesterday my three-year-old uttered three curse words after spending only a few days with my mom. It's amazing to me how much she influences my daughter after such a little time. We will not allow our children to go there alone again. I am willing to take that stand because I'm the adult now. In order to get to that point, I had to let my extended family go. There's 'seventy times seven' for them on the forgiveness part, but the protection side of me says 'no more.'"

There are many instances when it is our duty to prayerfully consider appropriate ways to protect our children from the influence of certain types of relatives:

- Those who are active in the occult.
- Those with a history of drunk driving.
- Those battling substance abuse.
- Those with a history of sexually abusing others.
- Those who leave loaded weapons around.
- Those who are racists.
- Those with addictions to pornography.
- Those with a history of breaking the law.
- Those who are careless, who don't understand the importance of supervision.
- Those who are cruel.

It may be entirely uncomfortable to say, "Uncle Joe, I can't let my children ride in a car with you because I can't trust that you won't drink and drive." However, letting your children ride in the car because you are too afraid to tell the truth is putting your children in danger. No matter how uncomfortable it may be, protecting children from harm is essential.

HOW TO PRESERVE THE RELATIONSHIP

Many of my fondest childhood memories involve spending time with my grandparents. Nearly every summer I flew to Ohio to visit my father's parents. We shopped, ate, went to amusement parks, and hung out at a lake together. We attended family reunions. My mom's parents lived close to where I grew up, so I visited them more frequently. My grandmother would tuck me in bed at night and treat me like a tiny queen, making cat-shaped pancakes and taking me out to lunch. My grandparents still wake up early, drink coffee, and read the newspaper every morning. What a blessing it is to have grandparents!

Because of that blessing, it is imperative that we do our best to preserve and foster our children's relationships with their grandparents, even if we might at times have to restrict visits. There are several practical ways do this:

1. Never speak ill of your children's grandparents. If at all possible, hold your tongue concerning your own issues with your parents. Say good things about them. Promote their strengths. Rejoice with your children when they share their love for their grandparents. There may come a time when your children are wiser and will ask you about discrepancies. If that happens, discuss the issues openly but with grace and love. Work through your own bitterness with the Lord so that it doesn't spill into the words you say about your parents. There may come a time when you have to say something, but if that time comes, season your words with grace. If you have to protect your children because of a grandparent's questionable behavior, use words like, "We love grandpa so much, but he is struggling right now. Will you help us pray for him?"

2. Teach your children forgiveness. Sometimes our children become privy to our relational struggles with our parents. They might witness their grandparents' unkind words and our subsequent pain. They may watch us deliberately try to wound their grandparents. But we can use personal failures like these as object lessons and say something to our children like, "I didn't use kind words with Grandpa. I need to ask his forgiveness. Will you forgive me too?" Modeling forgiveness for our children helps them forgive each other and their grandparents.

3. Identify the real enemy. Although Jesus said we very well might have enemies in our households because of our belief in him, the real enemy is not those who bring us turmoil or question our beliefs. The real enemy is Satan—the prince of the power of the air; the thief who comes to steal, kill, and destroy; the roaring lion seeking to devour us. The apostle Paul reminded us, "For our struggle is not against flesh and blood, but against the rulers, against the authorities, against the powers of this dark world and against the spiritual forces of evil in the heavenly realms" (Ephesians 6:12). If our parents don't know Christ, Satan is the cause of their blindness (see 2 Corinthians 4:4).

Instead of fretting over the pain parents inflict, remember that they are being infected by the one who is bent on destroying them. Our parents need our prayers. The object of our consternation should be Satan, not our parents. Even our children can join us as we pray that their grandparents' eyes would be opened to the beauty, tragedy, and victory of Jesus Christ. Be sure you remember who the real enemy is.

4. Love your parents. It seems simple, but the best way to preserve your children's relationship with their grandparents is to love your parents, to think of ways to bless them, to minister to them when they hurt, to listen, to offer to pray for them, to send them letters. If our children see our affection and love for our parents, they will cultivate a similar affection for them. Suzanne said, "I believe they will love their grandparents if you love them. I have tried to forgive and let the past be the past. This required a great deal of healing and honesty. For me, it was a blessing that I did that before I had kids." Loving our parents will be a great testimony to our children that, with God's strength, we can love even those who have hurt us most.

5. Encourage a connection. In our increasingly hypermobile society, there is a strong likelihood that your children don't live close to their grandparents. If this is the case, preserving their relationship with their grandparents takes time—and correspondence. Set up an e-mail account for your children. Share photos liberally. Teach your children basic letter-writing skills. When they receive mail, remind them how great it made them feel and how they could make their grandparents' day if they'd send a short letter. Send samples of your children's schoolwork and artwork to your parents. Let your kids call their grandparents on the phone.

6. Nix jealousy. When my mom spent dedicated time with my first child, I had a vague feeling of uneasiness about it. My mom enjoys Sophie's company. Seeing that opened up fresh wounds for me. The little girl in me screamed, *Why didn't you spend time with* me *when I was that age?* I was jealous. Sometimes I still am. As I've worked through my jealousy, I've come to understand that life does hold second chances and people do change. It's been beautiful to watch my mom spend time with my children. Yes, it's hard, but watching her engage in their lives has been very healing for me. It has helped me see her in a new light, with new eyes.

Suzanne could have been jealous of her daughter's relationship with her father. Instead, she rejoiced:

> The second time my daughter saw my dad, she went with him to the bank
> and spent the afternoon with him. I stood in the driveway in disbelief that
> I had just let my child drive off with my dad (not because I don't trust my
> dad, but because I never let her out of my sight), and it was glorious for
> my dad. He was thrilled. His relationship with my girl is a jewel in his and
> her crowns; they love each other, but it only came because I was able to
> forgive and pave the way for their relationship with my healing.

First comes healing. Then comes joy. When we are healed—and continue to be healed—from the past, we can learn to rejoice with our parents and their relationship with our children. We can demonstrate Jesus' love, stepping beyond our hurt and reveling in the joy of those who have hurt us.[1]

Our children desperately love their grandparents. When they part ways, our children weep. The children enjoy reminiscing about their visits when we look at vacation pictures. They jump up and down when their grandparents call. They send chatty letters, anticipate visits, and enjoy the attention and love they receive from their grandparents.

I'm thankful we've protected our children, but even more than that, I'm thankful we've been able to preserve the relationship our children have with their grandparents. Perhaps someday our children's close ties with their grandparents will serve as an avenue of healing between the generations. We pray that all three generations—grandparents, parents, and children—will live in holy reconciliation.

"Someone, Please Help Us!"

Finding a Mentor

Follow my example, as I follow the example of Christ.
—THE APOSTLE PAUL, 1 Corinthians 11:1

I haven't had a good track record with mentors. I remember once sending a card to a lady I wanted to mentor me. For weeks I didn't hear from her. When I saw her at church, she smiled at me. But other than that, nothing. Eventually I asked her husband about it, which thrust her out of lurkdom. "I don't do mentoring," she said. "I don't have my life together. I don't feel I can commit to it the way you may want me to."

In retrospect, I understand my error. A mentoring relationship is an organic thing, something that evolves naturally over time. The best mentoring experiences happen spontaneously, in the context of a growing friendship.

Not long after my initial failed attempt, I started meeting another lady from church to go walking. She had raised two sons who loved the Lord and were in full-time ministry. Throughout our long conversations, I asked her about mothering, being a wife, and growing spiritually. Even though I now live thousands of miles away from my mentor, I know I can still call her and reconnect.

The thing I've needed most as a pioneer parent is a mentor. Because I had no example of what it was like to be raised in a Christian home, I needed to see what that type of home looks like. I needed to watch other parents. Specifically, this is what I needed to see:

- conflict resolved in a healthy way
- how godly parents discipline their children
- forgiveness modeled and lived out
- a warm, inviting home
- what a marriage based on the foundation of Jesus Christ looks like
- how a family interacts spiritually
- how parents love their children

MENTORING INFLUENCES

It's imperative that we, as pioneer parents, learn from those who have walked the parenting path before us. Finding mentors can be tricky, though. It's not as easy as simply asking, "Will you mentor me?" It takes time. It takes the orchestration of the Holy Spirit. It takes prayer and persistence.

It's good, then, that there are many ways we can be mentored besides the conventional method. Here are two avenues that are readily available to you:

1. Learning by observation. Just watching a grandmother-type care for babies in the church nursery helps me. Seeing a father stoop low to comfort his crying son models Christlike parenting. Observing a harried mom patiently answering her inquisitive toddler teaches me to do the same. There will be times when we don't have mentors in our lives, but God still places people who love him everywhere—and each has the potential to influence us. Become an observer. Every act of kindness a mother does in a grocery store can be chronicled. Every grandmother rocking a baby to sleep has a lesson for us, such as being tender-hearted or slowing down enough to enjoy our children. I remember one woman who approached me in a store with a wistful look in her eye. "Enjoy your children," she said. "They won't be this young forever." Her advice sticks with me today.

2. Learning from books. When Sophie was born, I had a stack of parenting books on my nightstand. I was terrified to be a parent. I felt alone. But authors like Dr. James Dobson, Dr. Kevin Leman, Tedd Tripp, and Dr. Richard Swenson mentored me. (See the appendix for information about books that are particularly helpful for pioneer parents.) These folks elevated the occupation of parenthood in my mind. They shared their wisdom. They told me, through the printed word, that I was not alone. I am grateful for these mentors.

The Big Benefits of Mentoring

The New Testament model of mentoring (also called discipling) is beneficial to both parties. It has been said that no one truly grows spiritually by living apart from others in the Christian community. Mentoring is iron sharpening iron—in this case, parents sharpening parents. Because we pioneer parents grew up in homes we don't want to duplicate, it's important that we see Christianity modeled. In some ways, being healed from the past is not enough—sometimes we need to be re-parented. Mentoring accomplishes this.

Mentoring is beneficial because we learn better by example. I read books and books about how to potty train my son. Most left me frustrated or made me question my parenting ability. But then I watched a friend who refused to be worried about potty training, and it helped me relax. Within a few weeks—without the coercive use of jellybeans or chocolate on my part—my son was potty trained.

As a pioneer parent, I live with an evergreen fear that I'm doing things wrong, that I'll ruin my children. I try hard to be the best mom ever, only to feel myself lacking or berating myself when I make a mistake. I am thankful for a mentor who said, "Mary, you need to rest. God is in control. He loves your children more than you do. Do your best, but let God take care of everything else. Give yourself some grace."

Mentoring Elevates Your Vision of Parenthood

Other Christians have helped elevate my view of parenthood. Because I had a difficult childhood, I had no idea what *normal* was. Having other people in my life who hold parenting in high regard, who may have benefited from a more stable childhood, has shown me where I need to ask the Lord for help. My friend Suzanne agrees:

The example of other parents challenges me continually, not in trying to be like them, but in trying to keep God first. My sister has stated that the whole purpose of her homeschooling her children is so they

will know God and have an intimate relationship with him. That
challenges me. The model of other parents keeps me reaching higher.

Mentoring Answers Big Questions

As pioneer parents, we are full of questions, many unanswered. Here are a few
examples:

- Since I grew up in an abusive, overly strict home, why should I discipline my children?
- What happens if I have a problem with yelling at my children?
- My parents were emotionally distant. How do I form attachments with my children when I really have no idea how to do it?
- What do I do about my rebellious nine-year-old?
- How do I show my children in tangible ways that I love them?
- How do I train my children to be morally pure when I was impure?
- What do I do when my parents try to dissuade my children from the faith?
- How do I keep my marriage strong when my parents had multiple divorces?
- What happens if I've just become a Christian and I want to change my parenting methods?
- What tendencies exist in me that repeat the destructive patterns from the past?
- How do I teach my children about Jesus?
- What role should prayer have in my home?

The beauty of having mentors is that we can ask questions like these—as well
as hundreds of others—of someone who has trodden the path before us. If we
don't have mentors in our lives—if we have no one to turn to with our myriad
questions—then we can pray, asking the Lord to send us just the right person.

Mentoring Shows Us We're Not Alone

It's hard to express how much of a blessing it is to know that we're not alone. So
much of parenting these days is done in isolation. Communities have been shattered as we've become a transient society. Gone are the support systems of the
past. So instead of connecting with relatives or friends in the neighborhood, we

drive into our garages, shun our front porches (if we even have a front porch), and languish as parents within the four walls of our homes. Having mentors helps free us from isolation.

HOW TO FIND A MENTOR

Many pioneer parents wrestle with simply finding mentors. Finding people who will live life with us is difficult, so we need to embark on this undertaking with much prayer. Often, in our desire to learn how to parent our children, we rush out to find a mentor. We ask folks who are reluctant, and then we feel stupid afterward. Or we're too shy to approach someone who has her parenting act together, fearing she'll think we're inadequate or needy. Or mentors disappoint us. Or they move away.

Given the challenges, how do we find a mentor?

1. By looking within. Prayerfully reading through the first half of this book is one way to look within. Asking the Lord, "What are my weaknesses in parenting?" is another. Sometimes the Lord sends us mini-experts as mentors. For instance, I have a hard time emotionally connecting with my children. The Lord was gracious to send me Renee, who does a fabulous job connecting with her three daughters.

Also, I'd been wondering how I could integrate writing with family life. Around that time I met Sandi, who balances the same thing. Likewise, when I get lax about teaching my children life skills, I remember Leslie, who is the best mom I know at teaching her children responsibility. In order to recognize these mini-experts, though, we must know our own weaknesses and strengths as parents. The joy is that our strengths may serve as an inspiration for another struggling pioneer parent.

2. By looking in Christian settings. I've found most of my mentors in the local church. Through Bible-study groups, accountability groups, parenting groups, choir, and children's activities, I've been able to connect with a wide variety of parents. Parachurch organizations have also been a tremendous help: MOPS (Mothers of Preschoolers), Focus on the Family, Moms in Touch, FamilyLife, and Hearts at Home all are places I've been able to find mentors.[1]

3. By learning from in-laws. If your spouse is not a first-generation Christian, your in-laws can be a great source of encouragement. Jack's wife grew up in a stable

Christian home, so Jack often goes to his in-laws for advice. "The connection with my in-laws has been wonderful," he says. "They have a great balance of being there for us, yet they're not overinvolved in our lives." If your in-laws are not a good mentoring resource, begin praying that the Lord would bring older "parents" into your life who can encourage and strengthen you.

4. In everyday life. I've met other parents through the hustle and bustle of everyday parenting—on the playing field, at the grocery store, at PTA meetings, during parent-teacher conferences, at various gatherings and celebrations. For instance, our daughter Julia's soccer coach has been a tremendous example to us of how to have fun and enjoy our children. Part of the beauty and excitement of the Christian life is the fact that the Lord longs to surprise us. All we need to do is be aware, to ask him to show us snapshots of himself everywhere life takes us. If you are longing for mentors, start asking the Lord to surprise you with one. And then keep your eyes open.

What Mentoring Looks Like

There is no set protocol for mentoring. The process takes as many different forms as there are mentors. But the following elements are the same, no matter whom God has provided to be your mentor.

1. Spending time. Mentoring is living life with each other, sharing burdens, praying, opening yourself up to someone else. Perhaps that's the riskiest part of being mentored: laying your heart bare before the eyes and heart of another person. But the truth is, you won't grow if you try to grow in isolation. Your parenting will stay the same or stagnate if you don't dare to seek help.

Mentoring takes a lot of time. Don't expect to relate on a deep level immediately. Through shared meals, walks, phone calls and e-mails, and time spent just *being,* you will begin cultivating a relationship that can help you see your needs, your weaknesses, and your strengths. Don't begrudge how long it will take. Rest. Lean into the relationship. Enjoy.

2. Asking questions. Not only does mentoring involve your asking thousands of parenting questions, but it also involves allowing your mentor to ask you probing, and sometimes painful, questions. If you truly endeavor to grow as a parent, you must be willing to look at yourself and field difficult questions.

One mentor asked me, "Mary, are you spending too much time on the computer? Your daughter told me she misses your reading to her at night. She feels your writing is taking up too much time." He said it with much love, but it stung. The good part was that I was convicted enough to take action. That week I reduced my time on the computer and spent more time with my children, reading to them prior to bedtime again. The success of a mentoring relationship often depends more upon our ability to be questioned (and learning to work through our negative reactions) than our desire to have questions answered.

3. *Observing.* Mentoring is accomplished primarily through the vehicle of observation. We watch our mentors parent their children. We observe their marriages. We see how they interact with others. Conversely, we open ourselves up to be scrutinized. We allow ourselves to be watched. Mentoring, then, involves a hefty dose of vulnerability. It's never easy to open ourselves up to observation, particularly in parenting.

4. *Praying.* The best mentoring relationships involve copious amounts of prayer, both onstage and off, whether or not we're physically present. Mentors will stop what they're doing to pray for us. I've benefited from many over-the-phone prayers. I've reveled in my mentors' cyberprayers. I've wept as a mentor embraced me and prayed. Mentors also pray for us offstage—when we least expect it. Creating a mutually beneficial mentoring relationship also means that we pray for our mentors with the same passion and tenacity.

5. *Being teachable.* No matter how much you long to become a better parent, if you can't be taught or if you can't heed constructive criticism, there is really no use in pursuing a mentoring relationship. To grow, you must be thick-skinned (able to hear criticism even when it stings) and tender-hearted (teachable). Not everything a mentor shares with you will be correct or helpful. That's where your relationship with Jesus comes into play. Every piece of advice must be weighed and brought before him, before his eyes. If he confirms your area of weakness, then you can ask your mentor for help.

6. *Keeping Jesus at the center.* Never replace Jesus with another person. Suzanne said,

> Jesus doesn't want a mentor to replace him in your life, but he wants you
> to know the body of Christ as a priceless resource. There have been times

when I've mentored girls who placed me on a pedestal. When I failed, their faith faltered, because they were placing their faith in me (a quite fallible person) instead of Jesus Christ. No mentor is perfect. No mentor can fill us up the way Jesus can.

Several years ago I was on the brink of making a friend an idol. Whenever I had a problem, night or day, I'd call her. She'd patiently pray for me. She was there for me. But after a few months of my constant neediness, she said, "Mary, I am not Jesus. I can't fill you up. You need to learn to run to him first with everything.... I'm a poor substitute." She was right. I apologized and flung myself at the feet of Jesus, asking for his help. Instead of always running to my friend, I realized that Jesus would be there whenever I needed him.

I have a mentor now who loves me dearly. I didn't "acquire" her through persuasion. God must have known we needed each other because he placed us together. I'm grateful for her and can't imagine my life without her. I'm a better parent because of her influence on my life—her living, breathing, tangible example of how to parent well, pray deeply, and follow Jesus Christ fully.

Part III

Hope for the Future

Pioneer parents have hope. Because of the constant, helpful presence of the Holy Spirit, we can be confident that we won't be alone on this journey. Jesus comforted his disciples with these words before his crucifixion:

> And I will ask the Father, and he will give you another Counselor to be with you forever—the Spirit of truth. The world cannot accept him, because it neither sees him nor knows him. But you know him, for he lives with you and will be in you. I will not leave you as orphans; I will come to you. (John 14:16-18)

The Holy Spirit is with us always, so there is hope. Even when life is hard. Even if our children take detours. Even if our expectations of blissful parenting are shattered. There is hope.

17

"I Can't Wipe the Wilderness Off My Shoes"

Integrating God's Promise-Land Principle

The Promised Land always lies on the other side of a wilderness.
—HENRY ELLIS

The Promised Land. That place where milk and honey flow, where rest and stability, joy and peace abound. When God delivered the Hebrews from slavery in Egypt, he promised them a new home in a place they could call their own.

Today, as we try to parent our children well, we long for such a place—a place of beauty and security, peace and provision. Yet we forget all the pain it took for the Israelites to take possession of the Promised Land. They left behind slavery and oppression only to endure forty years of trials in the wilderness, followed by warfare against the nations that occupied their new home.

Such is the tenuous path we walk as pioneer parents. Many of us have been through oppression and trials growing up. We've faced ridicule, rejection, and sometimes abuse. When Jesus found us, we were delivered from our past. God's Spirit brought to mind his commandments so that we could live well in the land he gave us. Yet sometimes we still wander in the wilderness. Sometimes we stray from the land God has promised.

In parenting we resonate with the reality of warfare. Loving and training our children to be free in Christ has more to do with spiritual warfare than it does with our natural abilities as parents. With this in view, it's easy to understand our need for God's constant presence and guidance.

If you've seen the movie *The Ten Commandments,* with Charlton Heston starring as Moses, you'll remember Moses' vigor, as his staff turned the Nile River to blood and later parted the Red Sea, initiating the exodus of the Hebrews from slavery in Egypt. Full of life and vitality, Moses led the people toward the Promised Land. Yet the people rebelled against God. And Moses had a lapse when he didn't listen to the voice of God and struck a rock twice in anger instead of following God's instructions for providing water for the people (see Numbers 20:7-13). After forty years, when Moses had led the people to the edge of the Promised Land, the Lord told Moses he could mount a hill and gaze on the land, but he could not cross the river to go in. At the end of his life, Moses commissioned Joshua as the new leader in the presence of the children of Israel. Consider how his words relate to our parenting journey: "The LORD himself goes before you and will be with you; he will never leave you nor forsake you. Do not be afraid; do not be discouraged" (Deuteronomy 31:8).

For those of us on the cusp of entering our promised land, these words encourage us. We may never be able to enter the places our children will enter, but we can send them forth as God strengthens us.

THE BASIS OF OUR HOPE

Every pioneer parent has been on an arduous journey, fraught in the past with slavery but now characterized by God's precious deliverance. Now we have the opportunity to bless our children, to point them toward the promised land. How can we do that? By God's presence. Consider what his presence means to us as we pioneer this parenting journey:

1. The Lord himself goes before you. Believe it or not, God walks the paths we walk as parents. He walked with us when we lived with our own parents. He saw each tear, each frustration, each sin we committed, each hint of anguish. He went before us then, and he promises to go before us now.

Are you dismayed by parenting? Immobilized? Worried? Be encouraged. The Parent of all people walks the road before you. Like an explorer making his way through a dense jungle, God cuts away the sticker bushes that impede our path. He tells us where to step. He warns us about dangers. An omniscient God, he knows what happened yesterday, he is present with us this very moment, and he knows the future. In fact, he *holds* the future.

Sometimes God uses others in our lives to show us his nearness and his attentiveness to our daily needs. Recently, my daughter Sophie and I were in conflict, arguing about homework and chores. I lapsed into returning her angry words with a few cutting words of my own. Instead of deflating the arguments, I escalated them. Instead of embracing her—what she really needed from me—I emotionally walked away from her. She shared her frustration with Patrick, and he in turn shared Sophie's heart with me. I realized that I was duplicating a pattern I'd experienced in childhood, and eventually I was able to reconcile with Sophie.

"Sophie, I'm really sorry. I shouldn't have yelled. I shouldn't have walked away from you," I said. "I don't want you to think I'm not here for you or that I don't love you if we disagree."

"I'm sorry too, Mom," she said. "Sometimes I let my anger get the best of me too." We finished our conversation with a hug.

Because God goes before me, he was kind enough to use Patrick to show me the damage I was inflicting on Sophie—damage that could have followed her into adulthood if my words and actions had been left unchecked. God in his foresight stopped me.

2. The Lord will be with you. Not only does God go before us, he is with us right now. If we call him Lord and have surrendered our lives to the gospel of Jesus Christ, the Holy Spirit dwells within us every moment and is always available to help us. Even now I am in need of the Spirit's guidance. Last night I prayed for my son, whose favorite stuffed animal is lost. With huge tears we prayed that the Lord would help us find Jolly the dog. If we don't find Jolly, I need the sweet whisper of the Spirit to tell me how to love and parent my son through his tragedy. Even when I'm not sure how to navigate the parenting sea, I am sure the Holy Spirit will be with me, encouraging, instructing, and leading me down his path.

3. The Lord will never leave you. This is a promise from God that we need to internalize. He will *never* leave us. He will *never* forsake us. As pioneer parents, we may feel alone. Our lives may contrast greatly with the lives of other Christian parents. Our children may not walk the paths we want them to walk; they may wander. Even so, God will never leave us. He will not turn his back on us, utterly rejecting us. No matter how we fail at parenting, he will not throw up his hands in disgust and turn away.

4. So don't be afraid. I am insecure when it comes to parenting. I worry that my children might turn their backs on Jesus Christ. My insecurity comes from an insecure childhood, never being sure whether I was cherished, never quite knowing if I was safe. In adulthood, I fret that my children will experience my childhood. Whenever I make a mistake, I worry that I've messed up irrevocably. But the Scripture says, "Do not be afraid." In fact, the Bible is replete with the admonition to not be afraid (see, for instance, Genesis 26:24; Exodus 14:13; Joshua 10:25; Psalm 27:3; and Matthew 10:28). To enter the promised land in our parenting, we must lay our fears and insecurities at the feet of the One who bore all our shame and sin on the cross. Because of Jesus and his work on the cross, we have complete, unfettered access to God—the One who drives away all fear. With God, all things are possible. With his strength, we need not fear.

As I mentioned earlier, I had to work through a titanic fear when each of my daughters turned five. Seeing Sophie and Julia at that vulnerable age awakened my childhood ordeal with the boys who molested me. I worried that my daughters would be violated as I was, that they would bear the scars of sexual abuse. Although I kept a tight rein on my children—screening baby-sitters, getting to know the families of their playmates, not letting my children wander the neighborhood—I couldn't bear the thought that it could happen to them. So I prayed. And I asked others to pray for me. Eventually, the fear subsided. I am still vigilant. I am still aware that this world has predators. But God gave me the gift of peace despite my fears.

5. Do not be discouraged. When I read those four words, I smile. How can I *not* be discouraged? There are times when I feel as if I am sinking as a parent, when I can't seem to get anything right—when my eldest slams the door, saying, "It's not fair;" when my son cries, "I don't belong in this family" because he's the only boy. When my youngest sneaks and hides her behavior. Thankfully, the bookend for Deuteronomy 31:8 comes after many encouraging truths about God not leaving us or forsaking us, about his promise to always be with us—past, present, and future.

Because of him, I can fling off discouragement like a trench coat in the summer heat. Because he is the Great Encourager, I can lay my discouragement at his feet. Because his feet walked the craggy earth, he understands my painful journey.

PIONEER PARENTS IN THE PROMISED LAND

What do we do to become promised-land parents? How do we go about integrating the truth of God's presence into our parenting? Here are five ways:

1. Be set free and healed. The Israelites had to first be set free from slavery. Many pioneer parents are still living in the pain of their childhoods, and the pain has become a tourniquet around their hearts. Before we can endeavor to parent differently, we need to dare to have the Great Heart Surgeon free our hearts. Only he can remove the sting from the past. Consider the beauty of these words: "Then the LORD said to Joshua, 'Today I have rolled away the reproach of Egypt from you.' So the place has been called Gilgal to this day" (Joshua 5:9).

The Hebrew word for "Gilgal" sounds like the Hebrew word for "roll" (the action, not the bread). God is in the business of rolling away the reproach of our childhoods from us. Picture the pain from the past as a giant steel ball hitched between tired shoulders, forcing you to bend forward at the waist. For years you've carried the burden, but you have grown accustomed to it. Perhaps you've even nursed it. But its leaden heaviness is stooping your shoulders, pulling your eyes toward the earth, away from a heavenward glance. That ball affects everything—your worldview, your marriage, your friendships, your job, your parenting. It's time to decide whether you want to be released from your reproach, to have the weight roll off your shoulders.

Chronic emotional pain can become so ingrained in our hearts that we welcome it. There have been many times when I panicked because life was going too smoothly. I needed disaster. I needed pain. My security blanket was the heavy steel ball between my shoulders. But God knows we aren't fully alive if we are hunched over, contemplating our ankles. Even if we've become comfortable with our burden of pain, that doesn't mean it's good for us.

Let God remove the reproach of the past. Let him roll it off your shoulders so that freedom will reign in your parenting. The frustrating lie I've lived with is that parenting is all about what we do on the outside. That it's all about formulas and strategies, about what we say and when we say it. Methods have a place, but they can only have a healthy place when our hearts are clean and free from the encumbrances of the past. To parent well, we must first have new hearts. Only the healing touch of Jesus will save your parenting.

2. Remember how God rescued you. Once we allow God to roll the reproach of the past off our shoulders, it's important that we don't forget how he rescued us. One reason the generation of Israelites who left Egypt was not allowed to enter the Promised Land is that they forgot. They forgot the miracles that led to their deliverance. They forgot the mighty hand of God that parted the Red Sea. They forgot how God supplied bread from heaven and meat from the air. They forgot the pillar of fire that guided them. And in forgetting these signs, they forgot to recount the great stories to their children.

Moses warned the Israelites prior to their entering the Promised Land. He let them know how fickle they would be. We need a similar warning. We need to remember not to forget:

> [God] brought you water out of hard rock. He gave you manna to eat in
> the desert, something your fathers had never known, to humble and to test
> you so that in the end it might go well with you. You may say to yourself,
> "My power and the strength of my hands have produced this wealth for
> me." But remember the LORD your God, for it is he who gives you the
> ability to produce wealth, and so confirms his covenant, which he swore
> to your forefathers, as it is today. (Deuteronomy 8:15-18)

Not only are we to remember the great things God has done in our lives, but we are also to remember the Lord. We should revel in being rescued, but even more, we should revel in the Rescuer. Our children will catch more of our emphatic love for the Lord as we live our lives for him and worship him than if we only tell them things about God. To parent well, we must remember the Lord and endeavor to love him well in everyday life.

3. Tell stories. God gives all of us Gilgals—places where he rolls away the reproach of our upbringings. He calls us, like Joshua, to roll stones—the stones of our memories, the stones of our depravity, the stones of our loneliness. He calls us to erect a memorial with our pain so that we can point our children back to what God did. So we can give him glory. So we can give our children an authentic reality tale about how sin hurts people. We need to tell our stories of healing.

At Gilgal, God told Joshua to have the tribes of Israel gather twelve stones and build a memorial to God on the other side of the Jordan River. Why did God ask Joshua to erect this monument? Joshua explained why:

> In the future when your descendants ask their fathers, "What do these
> stones mean?" tell them, "Israel crossed the Jordan on dry ground." ...He
> did this so that all the peoples of the earth might know that the hand of
> the LORD is powerful and so that you might always fear the LORD your
> God. (Joshua 4:21-22,24)

Our testimony is like these stones—a narrative of God's provision, faithfulness, and miracles. In ancient times, stones were stacked as memorials to inform children, just as our testimonies do today.

Author Walter Wangerin Jr. affirms the use of stories for effective parenting:

> Storytelling conveys the realities and the relationships of our faith better
> than almost any other form of communication we have, for in story the
> child does more than think and analyze and solve and remember; the child
> actually experiences God through Jesus and through Jesus' ministry.[1]

4. Don't forget the Hand that fed you. As the Lord brings us to the parenting promised land flowing with milk and Honey Nut Cheerios, we may get so caught up in the beauty of life that we forget the Hand that poured the milk and cereal. Moses reminded the Israelites in advance:

> When you have eaten and are satisfied, praise the LORD your God for the
> good land he has given you. Be careful that you do not forget the LORD
> your God, failing to observe his commands, his laws and his decrees that
> I am giving you this day. Otherwise, when you eat and are satisfied, when
> you build fine houses and settle down, and when your herds and flocks
> grow large and your silver and gold increase and all you have is multiplied,

then your heart will become proud and you will forget the LORD your God, who brought you out of Egypt, out of the land of slavery. (Deuteronomy 8:10-14)

This is just as true for us today as it was for the slaves who were freed from Egypt. In order to remember the Lord, even in success, we must "praise the LORD your God for the good land he has given" us. A lifestyle of constant and consistent praise helps us remember God. Whether it is through our speech, our prayers, or the worship that permeates our songs, the simple and profound act of praising helps us remember.

Moses also said that we need to observe God's "commands, his laws and his decrees." To observe his commands is to obey them. When we obey the Lord, we cling to him all the more. In the act of obedience, we realize how needy we are, how much we lack faith. Modeling obedience, even when it is painful, is a lesson our children won't forget.

Instilling a passion for God in the next generations depends upon our willingness to model and teach praise and obedience to our children. An entire generation of Israelites failed to enter the Promised Land because they forgot the Lord. When the next generation neared its borders, God instructed Joshua to have the young men circumcised—a physical sign and reminder of God's covenant with his people. The desert generation did not praise God. They did not obey God. They did not teach their children about the ceremony of circumcision. The result?

The Israelites had moved about in the desert forty years until all the men who were of military age when they left Egypt had died, since they had not obeyed the LORD. For the LORD had sworn to them that they would not see the land that he had solemnly promised their fathers to give us, a land flowing with milk and honey. So he raised up their sons in their place, and these were the ones Joshua circumcised. They were still uncircumcised because they had not been circumcised on the way. (Joshua 5:6-7)

Pioneer parents must not forget—for the sake of our children. We need to share the greatness of God with them so they will be constantly aware of God's covenant with them as they go out into the world.

5. *Don't grumble.* God did allow two people of the older generation to enter the Promised Land. Two men who had circumcised hearts: Joshua and Caleb. Why? Because they dared to believe that God was powerful enough to conquer the nations that inhabited the land of Canaan. Moses sent twelve men to spy out the land. When they returned, ten of the spies grumbled, "We went into the land to which you sent us, and it does flow with milk and honey! Here is its fruit. But the people who live there are powerful, and the cities are fortified and very large.... We can't attack those people; they are stronger than we are" (Numbers 13:27-28,31). They spread discord among the entire nation, poisoning the people with small thoughts of God and big thoughts of their enemies. By the time Joshua and Caleb tried to convince everyone that God was more than able to prevail, it was too late.

What does this have to do with parenting? Grumbling poisons others. Believing that our circumstances are bigger than God's ability to overcome them has serious ramifications. Pioneer parents grew up in a negative environment, so we are prone to grumble. We lean toward seeing the world as dark and overpowering. We forget that God is bigger. I've seen it happen in my family. I'll grumble about why our missionary support is wavering. Instead of trusting the Lord to provide financially, I grumble. My children catch wind of my grumbling and grumble themselves. Like a contagion, grumbling begets grumbling. Pretty soon we have a house full of malcontents who start to believe that circumstances are bigger than God.

Psalm 78 is a retelling of Israel's sordid history. In the midst of it, the psalmist reminds us of the importance of praising, remembering, and storytelling. As we remember and tell stories, we are preparing hearts that are oriented toward God for the second, third, and fourth generations. When we instill faithfulness to the Lord in our children, we do so for our grandchildren and great grandchildren. Think about the power of these words:

> We will not hide them from their children;
>> we will tell the next generation
> the praiseworthy deeds of the LORD,
>> his power, and the wonders he has done.
> He decreed statutes for Jacob
>> and established the law in Israel,

which he commanded our forefathers
  to teach their children,
so the next generation would know them,
  even the children yet to be born,
  and they in turn would tell their children.
Then they would put their trust in God
  and would not forget his deeds
  but would keep his commands.
They would not be like their forefathers—
  a stubborn and rebellious generation,
whose hearts were not loyal to God,
  whose spirits were not faithful to him. (Psalm 78:4-8)

The Promised-Land principle is just that: preparing our children for the future so they can touch generations we'll never meet with the power and majesty of God.

"The Wolves Are Howling"

Preparing Your Children for the Big, Bad World

*The most important thing that parents can teach
their children is how to get along without them.*
—FRANK A. CLARK

I spoke with my friend Colleen last night. Her daughter is a sophomore in high school, something I can barely wrap my mind around. "When we hit the junior-high years," Colleen said, "life sped by. I can't believe my daughter's going to be a junior!" We spoke about what it would be like to have an empty nest, to not *see* our children every day. Later I wondered what it would feel like to launch my children into the big, bad world.

It's a process we parents hold in tension—nurturing our children in babyhood so they can grow up and be emancipated in young adulthood. We move from utter protection to complete relinquishing. H. Norman Wright cautions us along the journey:

Children pushed out of the home too soon can crash in flames.
But if we hold onto them too tightly, they usually end up with
an unhealthy adult dependence which hinders both personal and
relational maturity.[1]

As pioneer parents, we tend to err on the side of protection. We want so much to do this parenting thing "right" that we hold on to our children for dear life. The good news is that we can go with our children into adulthood—not physically but through our legacy, our influence. They will carry bits and pieces of us with them for the rest of their lives.

As Patrick and I discussed what we would like to leave our children with when they—*gasp!*—leave home, we discovered ten things:

1. God is for you. The world can be a scary place, full of people who are against us. An important truth to hold on to is that God is *for* our children. He, the Creator of the mountains and the sky, watches out for our children. The apostle Paul said, "If God is for us, who can be against us?" (Romans 8:31). Later, he clarified that nothing—not the present nor the future—can separate our children from the love of Jesus Christ (see Romans 8:38-39). As we parent our children, our underlying message should be that of grace—that God will carry them through any difficulty, that even when they walk through a Job-like week, God is still near. No difficulty can separate them from his love.

2. Life is not fair. It's a beautiful truth that God is for us, but it must be piggybacked upon a sadder truth: Life is not fair. I hear, "But that's not faaaaiiiir!" every day from my progeny, who love to place themselves as smallish judges of fairness. Even God in his dealings with humanity is not "fair" as we define the term. He allows the violent criminal who experiences a deathbed conversion the same amazing beauty of heaven as a soul who walked humbly with God for a lifetime. Throughout Psalms we hear the lament of David. Essentially he said, "Why do the bad guys get all the breaks? I'm doing my best to obey you, Lord, and things are falling apart. It's not faaaaiiiir!"

In this world, Jesus said, we'll have stress and worry and pain. He comforted his disciples by saying, "Take courage; I have overcome the world" (John 16:33, NASB). Still, it's difficult when bad people get ahead and good people encounter severe trials. It messes with our sense of fairness. The only way to reconcile the issue of fairness in our children's lives is to continually point them toward heaven. At the end of the ages, all wrongs will be set right. God, the perfect Judge, will lay everything bare. Every secret act of love we performed will receive the applause of the Scarred One. And every evil will be recompensed.

Included in our teaching about heaven should be the awesome recognition that we all deserve God's severe and merciless judgment. But because of Jesus' crucifixion, sinners can be made clean. That is not fair; and it's a good thing for us that God's sense of justice differs from our own.

Beyond teaching our children to think in terms of heaven, it is not wise to always be fair with them. If being fair is our goal as parents, then we aren't preparing them for the real world.

3. *Handling money well is important.* The statistics on consumer debt are staggering. Divorcing couples commonly mention finances as a major cause of the dissolution of their marriages. If we do not prepare our children to handle money well—and with a biblical perspective—we have not prepared them for the future. Because of the homes pioneer parents grew up in, we may not have been taught the biblical worldview regarding money and possessions. But for the sake of our children and their future, it's essential that we learn godly money management.

Patrick and I would not be debt free and living overseas as missionaries had it not been for two men who taught us biblical foundations for handling money: Randy Alcorn and the late Larry Burkett—both of whom have written tremendously helpful books. Larry Burkett taught us the importance of budgeting. Even our son, Aidan, when he had a windfall of money, told me, "Mommy, I'm going to get a piece of paper and write down my expenses so I know where my money goes." He's becoming a budgeter!

Burkett also taught us to make giving to God our first financial priority. In turn, we've taught our children the importance of tithing and giving. Every time our children get their allowance, they automatically set aside funds to give back to God.

Randy Alcorn taught us about having an eternal perspective in our daily lives. He opened our eyes to heaven and how we should give and live in light of eternity. Through his books, he taught us the importance of contentment. We try to model contentment with our children, delaying purchases, learning to repair what we have rather than replace it with something new. Our children don't always get what they want. Sometimes they have to work hard for things to understand the value of money.

Money encompasses so much of a young adult's life. Before we release one of our children from the nest, we need to teach them these lessons:

- God owns it all, so hold things and money loosely. They don't really belong to you.

- God is faithful and will provide for your needs.
- You can learn the secret of contentment.
- Someday you will give an account of your life, including how you spent the money God entrusted to you. Live in such a way that you will hear God say, "Well done, good and faithful servant!" (Matthew 25:23).
- Set aside the first portion of your income for God. Be willing to give, even when it means you'll have to do without some things.
- Budgeting is your best friend.
- Financial decisions made in haste will haunt you later. And remember: There is no such thing as "get rich quick."
- Honesty and integrity in your work are *always* preferable to cheating or lying to advance.
- Put aside savings for emergencies.
- Learning to trust God in finances takes a lifetime.
- You will balance a checkbook before you leave this house!
- Borrowing money makes you a slave to the lender. Avoid it, if possible.

4. We will love you no matter what. A parent's love is not dependent upon the child's actions. It may be excruciating to watch adult children make horrendous choices. Even so, welcome them home with open arms. While they are still sheltered under our roofs, it is imperative that we model Jesus' love—that whatever sin or failure may befall them, we still love them.

Keep in mind, though, that sometimes love is *tough,* as James Dobson says. Our loving may seem completely unloving to our children. A child who continually borrows money and then squanders it might yell, "You don't love me" when you cut him or her off financially. Yet, because you love your child, you will strive to teach him or her the necessary lesson of discipline. As our children grow, we must model this Godlike love—a love that disciplines in order to build godly character and welcomes the repentant son or daughter back with open arms.

5. Your choices mean something. Before they leave home, our children must know that their futures ride upon choices—critical decisions often made the first few years after leaving home. To prepare them now for the future, we must structure our homes in such a way that our children's choices mean something. The parenting strategy called Love and Logic is based upon the biblical truth that choices carry consequences. If a child forgets his lunch, the parent's responsibility—if she wants to see her child making wise choices—is to empathize but not bail her child out. Even now we can allow our children real-life consequences. As Jim Fay, founder of the Love and Logic Institute, says over and over in his talks, it costs our children far less to experience consequences when they are young and the stakes are lower than when they are older and their choices could lead to pregnancy, drug abuse, or death. Allowing for consequences when our children are young is one of the best gifts we can give them.

What are some tenets we want our children to know as they make adult choices?

- *Truth telling is paramount.* Even now, we should foster a love of truth telling in our children. If your child lies to you, make sure it brings a more serious consequence than if he or she had confessed the "crime." Lying and covering up take incredible amounts of energy, not to mention the distance it creates between our children and God.

- *Moral purity is absolutely essential.* Our entire beings belong to God, including our bodies. Because he sees us as precious, we ought to treat our bodies similarly (see 1 Corinthians 6:18-20). It is essential that we teach our children not merely what to avoid, but we also need to teach them their great value—that the Holy Spirit resides within them (if they know Christ). If children can internalize this truth, they will be more apt to make better choices when it comes to purity versus sexual sin, because obedience springs from the inside out.

- *God's forgiveness is free, but it is not cheap.* God is for our children, but his forgiveness came at an alarming price: the life of his Son. Helping our children understand the significance of the cross will help them make better choices—out of love for Jesus—in adulthood.

- *The best reference point is the Bible.* Throughout our parenting, we should be placing God's Word in the hearts of our children so that when they are older, they will recall key verses at key junctures. A friend of mine remembers the relentlessness of her mother in infusing Scripture into her life. "It often annoyed me, but the temporary annoyance was worth the effort on her part. She saturated us with Scripture. Mom would use sticky notes and index cards slipped into my books as 'bookmarks.' Her 'bookmark' method reminds me of how she used to slip green beans into our pizza."

6. It may hurt, but we will give you flight. The best gift we can give our children is the gift of letting go—to let them take flight, to let them learn dependence on God and interdependence on others. Watching our children struggle as adults can be excruciating, but we must let go.

The story has been told of a man who watched a moth try to break free from its cocoon. Moved with compassion for the moth, the man helped it along by tearing away the cocoon, eliminating the moth's struggle. The moth crawled out of the cocoon, wings crumpled and useless. Eventually, the moth died because its wings weren't strong enough. The struggle was necessary for the moth's wings to develop correctly. The author writes, "My misplaced tenderness had proved to be [the moth's] ruin. The moth suffered an aborted life, crawling painfully through its brief existence instead of flying through the air on rainbow wings."[2]

Part of parenting our children well is knowing when our tenderness will lead to their ruin. Our children must be allowed the grace to free themselves from the cocoon of childhood, or they will never fly. They need to struggle to survive. We must not rescue our children by interfering with the lessons God wants to teach them.

In the early 1800s, Ann Hasseltine's father had to allow for her struggle. Her fiancé, Adoniram Judson, asked for Ann's hand in marriage before they were to embark on missionary service to India. I wonder how I'd respond if I heard these words from one of my daughter's suitors:

> I have not to ask, whether you can consent to part with your daughter early next Spring, to see her no more in this world; whether you can consent to her departure, and her subjection to the hardships and sufferings of missionary life; whether you can consent to her exposure to the dangers of the ocean; to the fatal influence of the climate of India; to every kind of want and distress; to degradation, insult, persecution, and perhaps a violent death. Can you consent to all this, for the sake of Him who left His heavenly home and died for her and for you; for the sake of perishing immortal souls, for the sake of Zion, and the glory of God?[3]

We have to love our children enough to let them experience life's twins: joy and bitterness. If our children lay down their lives for Jesus Christ here on earth, we will spend an eternity enjoying them in heaven. This world is just a hiccup, a blip on the heart monitor of life. Someday, by God's grace, we'll dance with our children in the Celestial City.

7. *God made you the way you are for a reason.* The psalmist said that we are "fearfully and wonderfully made" (Psalm 139:14). God has made each human beautifully unique, with differing talents, callings, and hopes. I marveled when our second daughter, Julia, came along. She had blond hair instead of Sophie's brown, she thrived in social situations where Sophie was more contemplative, and she encouraged with her voice while Sophie encouraged through her pen. We are all unique, even within our families.

We are instructed to "train a child *in the way he [or she] should go,* and when he is old he will not turn from it" (Proverbs 22:6). That means we become astute observers of our children, always taking special note of God's gifting. We are to cheer on our children toward the way they were meant to go. Already I see my children heading in different directions. Sophie, articulate and artistic, may just be president someday. Aidan, the engineer, architect, and math lover, will likely design a space station on Mars. Julia, well, she'll no doubt use her gift of gab and encouragement to become a teacher or a mommy.

Besides steering our children toward the path God lays for them, we must also infuse a deep sense of joy about who they are physically, emotionally, and spiritually. Particularly with girls, a healthy body image is the key to surviving adolescence with purity intact. If we can hoe a path in our children's lives by offering encouragement that God has created each of them beautiful and unique, their lives will bear much fruit.

8. *God's call is radical.* Jesus called the disciples to leave everything and follow him. He told the rich young ruler to sell all he had and give the money to the poor. At the cross, Jesus beckoned us to come and die—to our agendas, our desires, our dreams. Before our children leave our homes, they must understand that the call of Jesus is costly. And it has eternal ramifications. As my family has ventured onto the mission field, it's been difficult to watch my children, particularly my eldest, struggle with the calling on their lives—a calling that uproots them from everything familiar, away from every friendship, away from a wonderful church and a relatively easy life. When Sophie turned eleven, I wrote her a letter to share the truth that the call of God is radical and eternal:

On this, your eleventh birthday, I want to encourage you to walk in King David's shoes. He wanted to erect an altar to the Lord and worship him. He approached a man about some land. He wanted to buy it to make the altar there, but the man, Araunah, said that David could have the land for free. David responded this way: "No, but I will surely buy it from you for a price, for I will not offer burnt offerings to the LORD my God which cost me nothing" (2 Samuel 24:24, NASB).

Sophie, this year as we move away from everything comfortable, you have the unique opportunity to offer something to God that costs you everything. Sacrifice is hard. David could easily have taken the land for free and then offered his sacrifices to God, but then they wouldn't be difficult.

Sometimes God asks us to do hard things for the sake of his Kingdom. You now have a choice—to understand that life is a series of humbling circumstances. We may not always love where God takes us, and we may not like it or understand his ways, but eventually, I pray you'll understand what a privilege it is he's given you to offer your whole self to him, no matter how hard it is or at what cost.[4]

Following Christ is costly. As parents we must first model our own receptivity to his call to the nth degree. As our children see us drop our nets and follow Jesus, they'll understand, in a pragmatic way, what it means to live radically for him.

9. *We are all part of something bigger than ourselves.* Life is not all about us. It's about the eternal Kingdom of God—advancing it, embracing it, sharing it with others. It is my hope that our children will intrinsically understand this because of the choices Patrick and I have made, or perhaps, more fitting, by the mistakes we've made. Life is not about acquiring things or using others for our benefit. It's not best lived in selfishness. True life is lived in light of eternity. Author Randy Alcorn often shares this truth: "All of us are made for a person and a place. Jesus is the person. Heaven is the place."[5] If our affections bend toward Jesus and his home in heaven, our lives will spill into others' lives, advancing the expanding Kingdom of heaven. As we rejoice in the trials God places in our paths and look forward to eternity, our children will catch that same spirit of giving up earthly things for the sake of gaining eternal rewards.

10. We are all pioneers—leaving is inevitable. This week I discovered a word that came from one of those word-a-day e-mail lists: *momism*. Someone coined it in the mid-nineteenth century. It means "to have an excessive attachment to one's mother." Conversely, it means "excessive mothering or overprotection." Many of our families suffer from *parentism*. Either our children are too attached to us as they leave (maybe!) the home, or we are guilty of overprotection.

We are all pioneers, though, and we must venture beyond what is comfortable. Life is more adventurous when we view it for what it is: uncharted territory. We are walking a new path with our children, deviating from the path we ourselves walked as children. Our children grow up to become pioneer adults, able to speak to a generation we'll not be able to reach. They are the arrows we shoot into an unknown future. But first, we must pull the arrows out of our quivers, stretch our bowstrings taut, and release our children into the wind.

God has entrusted our children to us. We are stewards of them from infancy to adulthood, from dating to marriage, from dabbling in hobbies to establishing a career. Life rushes by far too quickly. But lessons our children learn in childhood will—we pray—become the foundation for their adulthood as they make their way in this big, bad world.

"We're in This Together"

Encouraging Other Pioneer Parents

We urge you, brethren, admonish the unruly, encourage
the fainthearted, help the weak, be patient with everyone.
—1 THESSALONIANS 5:14, NASB

I sat across from a cherished friend in a small breakfast restaurant. I remember how the table looked, round and small, and I remember her piercing, condescending words. "The way you parent Sophie is not good."

She brought up an incident in which Patrick and I were trying in vain to remove a splinter from Sophie's foot. Sophie was screaming, and we were at a loss as to what to do. In retrospect, I think I would have done things differently and let the sliver rest a bit. Even so, my friend's words crushed my resolve and ate away at my parental confidence. For two years I believed her words. In fact, her words morphed into a full-fledged chorus of "You're not a good parent. You're no good. You're damaging your children."

It wasn't until I moved to another state and attended a new church that I began hearing new friends say things such as, "Your children are a joy to have in Sunday school. You and Patrick have done a great job. I love how obedient and happy your children are." Removed from my critical friend and buoyed by the encouragement of these new friends, the cloud over me lifted, and I began to see myself as a good parent.

We all have critics. For pioneer parents, our critics can be as close (and as damaging) as our own parents or siblings. Receiving discouraging criticism from those who are supposed to encourage us steals our joy. Because of critics, familial or not, it's important that we minister in the opposite spirit. If others belittle us or say damaging things to us about our parenting, then we can, by God's grace, refrain from returning the favor, *and* we can determine to *encourage* rather than discourage fellow pioneer parents. Here are a few of the things we can do to become encouragers:

1. Seek God's refreshment. So much of my life has been wrapped up in seeking the approval of others that I've had to learn the secret of seeking God's rejuvenation. Before I can hope to encourage other pioneer parents, I must first be refreshed. One of my favorite verses is Jeremiah 31:25: "For I satisfy the weary ones and refresh everyone who languishes" (NASB). To *languish* is "to lose or lack vitality, to droop." How often that is true of me! This parenting journey is full of places of weariness—places where I'd die from keen thirst if I didn't ask for God's refreshment. He promises to refresh me when I languish, just as a dousing of water revives a drooping sunflower.

Interestingly, God uses paradoxical means to refresh us. Sometimes he sends a direct rejuvenation from his heart to ours. We worship, and he fills us. We pray, feeling his presence. We read words about him and are strengthened. But he also satisfies us as we refresh others.

Last summer was full of intense moments of discouragement for our family. Even our children have not escaped the constant stress. Preparing to move our entire household overseas with all the logistics such an endeavor entails completely wore down my husband, Patrick, and me. Worrying through raising financial support, selling a house, finding a house thousands of miles away, we languished, drooped. One weekend we piled our children into our minivan and drove several hours to do support raising. Initially the children bickered, but eventually things settled down as we watched the East Texas hills undulate before us. As we neared our destination, I prayed, "Lord, help us to stop focusing on ourselves. Use us to minister to others."

We spent the weekend listening to others. Once in a while we'd share our own needs, but mostly we prayed for those who were hurting. As so often happens in God's paradoxical kingdom, we drove away refreshed. Through our act of encouraging others, God encouraged us. The Scriptures are true: "A generous man will prosper; he who refreshes others will himself be refreshed" (Proverbs 11:25). If we long for God's rejuvenation, we need only seek him and ask him to refresh others through us.

2. Remember where you came from. If we are to encourage other pioneer parents, it's important to remember where we've come from. We need to examine our journeys, recounting God's faithfulness along the way. Yesterday Patrick and I spent several hours with friends at the beginning of their parenting journey. They have a one-year-old who toddles happily through their home. How quickly I forget what parenting was like back then—the diapers, the sleepless nights, the constant giving of your attention. To encourage others, I need to remember. And in remembering, I can then offer encouragement.

Many pioneer parents struggle, wondering if they are doing a good job with this crazy task of parenting. They worry constantly about making mistakes. The word *insecurity* defines them. Knowing this, we frequently need to tell one another what we do well. We need to notice one another's triumphs. We need to praise one another's children.

3. Do unto others. How would you like to be encouraged? What would have been beneficial to you as you started down the path of pioneer parenting? In whatever ways you love to be encouraged, strive to encourage other parents in similar ways. I would have loved to have a date night with my husband when my children were little, but we often couldn't afford baby-sitting. Once in a while, a friend would tell us to go out, offering to baby-sit for free. Now we can do that for other parents.

Having someone notice that my children knew they were loved started a freedom revolution in my heart and set me on a path toward healing. Now I can observe other pioneer families and offer specific encouragement. Isn't that God's intent for humankind? That he would bless us so that we can bless others and point them to him (see Genesis 12:2-3)? As pioneer parents, we walk a path of complete faith, parenting in ways we were never parented, going places with our children our parents never walked. And yet, in that pioneering journey, God blesses us so that we can be a blessing to others.

4. Remember that every journey is different. No parenting journey is the same. One parent may assign great importance to attachment in parenting. Another may emphasize compassion over discipline, while others value discipline over compassion. There is no one right path. Embracing diversity in parenting is a key component for encouraging other pioneer parents. Whether we disagree with or herald a particular parenting method is not the issue. Seasoning our words with grace and joy is. We always have the choice to encourage.

One friend recounted a frustrating occasion, saying that she enjoyed spending time with a certain friend of hers, except for one thing. "Since we have children the same age, my friend feels it's her duty to inform me as to how I should parent differently. She points out methods that work for her children. It makes me feel judged." Remember: Advice is welcome only when others ask for it. Volunteering "helpful" advice only makes fellow pioneer parents feel judged and inadequate.

5. *Be specific about praise.* "You're a great parent!" is a nice thing to say, but it's not very helpful. If we endeavor to encourage other parents, we must become observers over a period of time and then offer specific encouragement, such as:

- "I admire the way you teach your children about Jesus before they go to bed."
- "I love how your children listen to you when you speak—that you don't raise your voice to be heard."
- "Your children love each other and seem to resolve conflict quickly. What's your secret?"
- "I've noticed how respectful your children are when I call you. Can you give me some tips to teach my children phone manners?"

The last two pieces of encouragement add something: a request for advice. Perhaps the most encouraging thing fellow pioneer parents can hear is a question that seeks their input. By asking for advice, we not only validate other parents, but we give them the joy of telling us about their own journeys. And in the midst of that, we are encouraged.

6. *Remember grace.* Grace—God's unmerited favor—should be the foundation of our encouragement. Because we have received a superabundance of God's pardon, forgiveness, and favor, we, in turn, can extend that same grace to others. No pioneer parent is perfect. I am quite aware of my own failures. So I encourage others from a position of meekness, knowing that I am a fellow parenting pilgrim.

7. Use different means to encourage. Encouragement takes many forms, so be creative. Because God encourages us in various ways, we can follow in his steps and do likewise.

- *Listen.* Pull up a chair, shut out whatever might distract you, and give a fellow parent your ears. Let him vent. Let him wonder. Validate him as he speaks. Restate what he's said. Look him in the eye. Empathize. Refrain from giving advice. Just listen.
- *Pray.* There are many ways to pray—over the phone, by e-mail, individually, as the parent comes to mind. And don't forget, you can pray as you place your hands on a struggling parent's shoulders.
- *Send a note.* Spend time considering words and Scriptures that would encourage another parent, then write them down in a note and send it.
- *Speak encouragement.* Direct, person-to-person encouragement can be life changing. If you admire something a parent does, or if you want to share God's faithfulness with her during a trying time, go ahead and say what's on your heart.
- *Give a gift.* Consider your struggling friend and what would specifically encourage him. Has he mentioned something he'd really like? Demonstrate God's extravagance and give freely.
- *Give time.* Time is such a precious commodity, so show a pioneer parent how much you love her by spending time with her.
- *Share the load.* Offer to baby-sit. Hire a housekeeper to clean a friend's house, or offer to clean out the garage. Bring meals to suffering families. Schedule play dates for their kids.
- *Give financially.* Some of the greatest times Patrick and I have shared are when we've given money to needy families. At times we've given anonymously. At other times we've let them know that the gift came from us. We've taken others out to dinner—all for the sake of showing Christ's love and imparting courage to those who struggle.

8. Pray about being a mentor. In the midst of encouraging other pioneer parents, pray about whether the Lord would have you be a mentor. If you've experienced the benefits of having a parenting mentor, consider giving back by mentoring another couple. If you haven't had the experience of being mentored, still consider being one. None of us quite feel equipped for the title of mentor, yet

God promises that he is our strength in weakness. He is the ultimate Mentor and will mentor us as we mentor others.

Often you'll find that the Lord will place people in your path—folks who ask for advice, who lean on you for understanding. This organic relationship, though not defined formally as mentoring, really *is* mentoring. Be alert to the people God places in front of you. Be available.

Although I still remember the discouraging words of my critical friend, I recall more often the words of those who have endeared themselves to me through encouragement. Maturity comes when we're able to use the discouraging words from others as springboards to becoming parents who encourage. Imagine starting a revolution of rejuvenation among pioneer parents by giving those who struggle a much-needed drink of refreshment. Not only will your words and actions spur pioneer parents toward greater parenting, but they will also trickle down to bless pioneer children, who will then take the grace of Jesus Christ to the next generation.

20

"What Now?"

Parenting with an Eternal Perspective

So we fix our eyes not on what is seen, but on what is unseen.
For what is seen is temporary, but what is unseen is eternal.
—2 CORINTHIANS 4:18

The elementary-school principal smiled as he looked at the passel of parents sitting in front of him. "I just have one piece of advice for y'all," he drawled. "It goes by awful fast."

I watched my five-year-old, who was sitting prim and proper with mortarboard and tassel cocked to one side, her blond hair jutting out this way and that. The principal was right. Just yesterday it seems, Julia toddled toward me, arms open, smile wide, diaper fitting loosely. Life speeds by. If we don't take time to consider its brevity, we'll cease living for things that last—like the souls of our children or the glory of the One who created them.

Having an eternal perspective will change every aspect of your life—finances, time, possessions, relationships, and, yes, even parenting. What is an eternal perspective? It is living for the other world rather than this one. It is counting God's smile as more important than another person's smile. It is living each day as if it were our last, making decisions that will one day garner a "Well done, good and faithful servant!" (Matthew 25:23).

Consider the apostle Paul's take on having an eternal perspective:

Therefore we do not lose heart. Though outwardly we are wasting away, yet inwardly we are being renewed day by day. For our light and momentary troubles are achieving for us an eternal glory that far outweighs them all. So we fix our eyes not on what is seen, but on what is unseen. For what is seen is temporary, but what is unseen is eternal. (2 Corinthians 4:16-18)

The things that matter in this life and the next are the unseen things—loving our children, giving to others in secret, taking the last place, considering others more important than ourselves, worshiping our Creator. These intangibles constitute an eternal perspective.

So often, though, parents run frenetically through life like gerbils on an exercise wheel, never stopping to consider whether we are living for the country we were made for: heaven. When the author of Hebrews wrote of great people of faith, he spoke of their allegiance to the far better country. "Instead, they were longing for a better country—a heavenly one. Therefore God is not ashamed to be called their God, for he has prepared a city for them" (Hebrews 11:16).

The enemy of our souls has duped many parents, making them believe that what they see is all that matters. Yet God's Kingdom is unseen, and we are his ambassadors, representing that unseen Kingdom to those around us. Far too many of us are poor ambassadors. "Imagine an ambassador who leaves his country to live in another nation hostile to his own," writes Randy Alcorn. "Naturally, he'll want to learn the language, see the sights, eat the food, become familiar with the people and culture. But suppose he fails to draw the line. Suppose he becomes so engrossed in this country's customs and philosophies that he gradually assimilates into it.... At best, he becomes incapable of serving his true country. At worse, he may actually betray it. He may defect."[1]

Having an eternal perspective means that we will train our children to live for heaven and the glory of Jesus. We do this by invitation and modeling, not by mere words. We do this in spite of our upbringing. We whisper words of eternity even if our parents berated us about being no earthly good. No matter what obstacles we face, be they parental or personal or circumstantial, above all we must impart to our children a holy fear of God, a love for his advancing Kingdom, and a longing for heaven that defies cultural logic.

GAINING AN ETERNAL PERSPECTIVE

What does parenting with an eternal perspective look like? Here are some distinguishing characteristics:

1. Suffering takes on new meaning. As we suffer and our children suffer for their stand for Jesus Christ, we can infuse suffering with new meaning. Even when we suffer from illness, financial difficulties, or relational angst, we can teach our children to focus on heaven and how amazing it will be. We can remind them that God records every tear: "Record my lament; list my tears on your scroll—are they not in your record?" (Psalm 56:8). We can choose to rejoice in trials, to sing when life is dark, to demonstrate that there is more to life than trudging through pain.

We can comfort our children by telling them that their pain is not in vain, that God watches how we respond to it and will eventually reward our faithfulness. "The more faithful to God we are in the midst of our pain, the more our reward and joy," writes Christian author and speaker Joni Eareckson Tada. "Whatever suffering you are going through this minute, your reaction to it affects the eternity you will enjoy. Heaven will be more heavenly to the degree that you have followed Christ on earth."[2]

2. Being faithful reaps rewards. As we point our children to the beauty of heaven, we can teach them the benefit of being faithful to God, as well as the detriment of turning their backs on him. When I read the following verses, I imagine a great heavenly bonfire in which all my good intentions, feigned acts of obedience, snippets of lip service, and lack of faithfulness get devoured by holy flames.

> If any man builds on this foundation using gold, silver, costly stones,
> wood, hay or straw, his work will be shown for what it is, because the Day
> will bring it to light. It will be revealed with fire, and the fire will test the
> quality of each man's work. If what he has built survives, he will receive his
> reward. If it is burned up, he will suffer loss; he himself will be saved, but
> only as one escaping through the flames. (1 Corinthians 3:12-15)

Part of instilling an eternal perspective in our children is helping them see the importance of a life well lived—a life that won't be consumed by fire, a life that beckons eternal rewards.

3. Modeling an attitude of worship that our children will imitate. I remember a sermon I heard fifteen years ago. "Worship is our primary occupation in heaven," the pastor said. "What are you doing now to prepare for that job?" If we are living in light of eternity, our lives will be permeated with adoration and worship. If we long for heaven, we will be consumed with worship, since that will be the air we breathe on the streets of glassy gold. Worship, giving God the praise he is due, is something our children will catch from us. We must model an attitude of worship, particularly when our lives are painful or things are out of control. Even last summer, as Patrick and I readied our family for a huge move overseas, I let the craziness of life overwhelm me. Finally, I put a CD of worship music in the stereo and began to sing. The words and the music helped remind me that God is on his throne and that he is in control.

Knowing how worship will look in heaven will help us model the same worship on earth, so we can, as a family, prepare for our eternal occupation. Worship involves the following:

- *A recognition of God's power, worth, and honor.* "The twenty-four elders fall down before him who sits on the throne, and worship him who lives for ever and ever. They lay their crowns before the throne and say: 'You are worthy, our Lord and God, to receive glory and honor and power, for you created all things, and by your will they were created and have their being'" (Revelation 4:10-11).

- *A chorus of the nations.* "Then I heard every creature in heaven *and on earth* and under the earth and on the sea, and all that is in them, singing: 'To him who sits on the throne and to the Lamb be praise and honor and glory and power, for ever and ever!'" (Revelation 5:13). This truth should stir us all to be missionaries—wherever that may be—for his glory.

- *A declaration of his salvation.* "After this I looked and there before me was a great multitude that no one could count, from every nation, tribe, people and language, standing before the throne and in front of the Lamb. They were wearing white robes and were holding palm branches in their hands. And they cried out in a loud voice: 'Salvation belongs to our God, who sits on the throne, and to the Lamb'" (Revelation 7:9-10).

4. Making the most of our days. Having an eternal perspective helps us gauge our daily lives. As Julia's school principal said, life "goes by awful fast." Thinking in terms of what will last into the next life helps us engage fully in the lives of our children. It helps us make good decisions about how involved our families will be in church, activities, and sports. It helps us honor one another even when we are irritated. The apostle Paul said, "Be very careful, then, how you live—not as unwise but as wise, making the most of every opportunity, because the days are evil. Therefore do not be foolish, but understand what the Lord's will is" (Ephesians 5:15-17).

We've all heard it said that most deathbed regrets have to do with not having spent enough time with one's family rather than not having made enough money. One minute after we die, we'll realize how silly some of our choices were. The key is to live life fully dedicated to Jesus Christ and fully engaged in the lives of our children, for his glory. Christian author Randy Alcorn urges,

> As there will be no second chance for the unbeliever to go back and live
> his life over again, this time accepting Christ, so there will be no second
> chance for the believer to go back and live his life over again, this time
> serving Christ. *Now* is our window of opportunity. *Now* is our chance to
> follow Christ, speak the truth and reach out to the needy in love. *Now* is
> our chance to invest our lives in eternity.[3]

5. Understanding that someday life really will be fair. As parents steering our children toward heavenly things, we are faced regularly with the "it's not fair" pleas of our children. Someday, though, life *will* be fair. All good deeds will be praised, and all wrongs will be righted under the holy scrutiny of the Supreme Judge:

> Then I saw a great white throne and him who was seated on it. Earth and
> sky fled from his presence, and there was no place for them. And I saw the
> dead, great and small, standing before the throne, and books were opened.
> Another book was opened, which is the book of life. The dead were
> judged according to what they had done as recorded in the books. The sea
> gave up the dead that were in it, and death and Hades gave up the dead

that were in them, and each person was judged according to what he had done. Then death and Hades were thrown into the lake of fire. The lake of fire is the second death. If anyone's name was not found written in the book of life, he was thrown into the lake of fire. (Revelation 20:11-15)

These cadenced words, written by the apostle John, Jesus' closest friend on earth, should cause us all to pause, to consider how we are raising our children, how we are living our lives, how we are viewing this life. As pioneer parents, we are walking a brand-new road, which at times is unpaved and rocky. And yet we are all walking on a path to the end of time, when we will see the face of God.

The hopes and prayers of pioneer parents are that we would be a Kingdom-minded generation, that through the wooing of the Holy Spirit, our parents would surrender their lives to Jesus and our children would take his baton forward on smoother roads. May it be that we all walk on heavenly roads, arm in arm, generations entwined.

As a fellow pioneer parent, I can think of no greater joy.

Discussion Guide

Questions for Reflection
and Growth

This guide is designed for a variety of uses: personal reflection, discussion with a prayer partner, conversation over coffee with a few friends, small-group study, or Christian education in a local church setting. Many of the questions are designed to help you relate the material of the chapter to your own life in a practical way. For further study, you may wish to examine more closely the Scripture passages that are presented in each chapter.

Introduction: God Is Bigger Than Our Past

1. When you have told the story of your upbringing to other people, how have they responded? How did their responses affect you?
2. What part of the author's story resonated with you? Why?
3. Read Jeremiah 31:11. Recount how you think God redeemed you from those stronger than you. What does God's redemptive work mean to you?
4. What fears did you have when you held your first child? How did your upbringing factor into those fears?
5. Are you at the place where you can thank God for your upbringing? Why or why not?
6. Read Psalm 41:1-3. In what ways do these verses reflect your past?

Chapter 1: "I'm Afraid of the Sky Ghost!"

1. In what ways was your childhood safe? How was it unsafe?

2. What role did grace play in your upbringing? What role does it play in your life today?
3. Did you feel cherished as a child? Why or why not?
4. What rules from your childhood home stand out to you today? Which rules were beneficial? Which were painful or destructive?
5. Did your parents give you the freedom to fail? Recount an experience in which you were not given the freedom to fail. How did that incident make you feel? How does that affect your parenting choices today?
6. Do you believe you are a good parent? Why or why not? Who, if anyone, has encouraged you in your parenting? When? If so, how did that help you?

Chapter 2: "I'd Rather Forget the Past"

1. In a personal journal or in conversation with a group of trusted friends, take laps around your childhood. Thank God for each year and ask him for his perspective on your upbringing. When you're finished with your laps, reflect on how this made you feel. Exposed? Vulnerable? Free?
2. To use the author's "key" metaphor, are you hiding the key to the dark closet of your past, afraid to give it to the Lord? If so, why? What has prevented you from giving God the key?
3. When has God used a friend or counselor to help you peel away the layers of your past? What were the results?
4. Where do you find yourself between the extremes of "overproclaiming" and "clamming up"? What would a trusted friend say about you? Do you say too much or too little? Explain.
5. When you look back on your childhood, what patterns of personal sin emerge?

Chapter 3: "But You Don't Know How Bad Things Were!"

1. Jesus asked the paralytic if he wanted to get well. He asks the same question of you today. Do you want to get well? Why or why not?
2. Describe the process of emotional healing you've experienced in the past five years. What were the most significant turning points?

3. How does the story of Joseph relate to your story? What meaningful similarities are there, if any?

4. When have you failed to return to God? What specific emotional injuries do you blame God for?

5. Has anyone ever told you that you are afraid of abundance? If so, do you agree that you tend to shy away from blessings? Why?

Chapter 4: "I Won't Become My Parents!"

1. Which, if any, of the author's self-defeating vows are similar to ones you have made? What has been the outcome in your life of making such vows?

2. In what ways have you vowed to protect your heart? Would your spouse or children say you've erected a protective wall around your heart? Why or why not?

3. Who in your life can you trust enough to help you explore your destructive vows?

4. What do you gain from your vows? Why do you keep them?

5. Describe a time when you let go of a destructive vow by relinquishing your control and allowing God to take over. What was the outcome?

Chapter 5: "What About the 491st Time?"

1. Who in your life is hardest to forgive right now? Has reconciliation taken place in this relationship? Why or why not?

2. When you remember your childhood, what is your primary emotion? Fear? Sadness? Anger? Glimpses of joy? Why is this your primary emotion?

3. How does understanding the depth of Jesus' forgiveness help you today in your journey to forgive those who have wronged you?

4. Write a letter of forgiveness to the person or persons who came to mind in question 1. Describe the pain of the incident and release the person from the penalty of his or her sin against you. How did you feel after writing the letter? (Don't send the letter unless you know God is urging you to do so.)

5. In what ways do you see your past as a gift?

Chapter 6: "It's Time to Leave Home"

1. Referring to the author's story about loving her mother too much, honestly assess your relationship with your parents. Do you love them too much? too little? Why or why not?
2. When have you experienced being "without honor" in your extended family? In what ways have you suffered persecution? What was your response?
3. Jack mentioned a time when he decided to stop riding the fence between his wife and his mother. "It meant defying the one no one defies," he said. Have you ever ridden the fence between your spouse and one or both of your parents? If so, what happened as a result? Would your spouse say you value him or her over your parents?
4. What have you purposefully done to promote oneness in your marriage? In what areas are you not one with your spouse? What practical steps can you take to grow in these areas?

Chapter 7: "But My Parents Drive Me Crazy"

1. What has been the most difficult part of seeking to honor your parents? What has made this so difficult?
2. What prevents you from telling your parents the truth?
3. Read Mark 3:31-35. How does this scripture help you define who is to receive your highest allegiance?
4. Bethany talked about releasing her parents from expectations. What expectations do you have for your parents that remain unmet? How can you work on lowering your expectations? How might that improve your relationship with your parents?

Chapter 8: "I Just Can't Do This Parenting Thing"

1. When have you felt that you were weakest as a parent? In those times, have you experienced God's strength? If so, in what ways?
2. What does parental success look like to you? Make a list of five traits that typify a successful Christian family. According to the author, why is merely trying to succeed in parenting a shortsighted goal?

3. In what ways does your system of child rearing reflect your rebellion against the way you were raised?

4. How has your quest to become a perfect parent backfired? What role do authenticity and brokenness play in your parenting today?

5. Recall a time when you sought God for specific answers in your parenting. What happened? Now consider another time when you fell at his feet, wanting *him* more than the answers. How did you feel in the midst of that time?

Chapter 9: *"Why Not Just Give Me Some Rules and Be Done with It?"*

1. How does the sandwich metaphor help you understand the way God strategically placed you in your extended family?

2. In what ways has marriage helped you become more selfless? In what ways has parenting helped?

3. Christianity is a call to die to self. What areas of self do you sense God is calling you to hand over to him?

4. Write out a prayer to God about your children, covering emotional, physical, and spiritual bases. What role does prayer have in your day-to-day parenting?

5. The author speaks of "campaign parenting." How have you campaign-parented this past week?

6. The author states, "Purposeful parenting proceeds from healed hearts." In what areas of your life do you see your need for divine healing?

Chapter 10: *"Even When They're Whining—or I Am?"*

1. What would gratitude-based parenting look like in your home?

2. In what ways have you blamed your parents or your children for your parenting failures?

3. How has comparing yourself to other parents sabotaged gratefulness in your life?

4. In what ways has God changed your minor-key dirge into major-key praise of him?

Chapter 11: "But I'm Not a Handyman!"

1. Growing up, did you feel loved? Why or why not? What role does love play in your parenting today?
2. In what ways have you incorporated Scripture into your daily routine with your children?
3. How do you typically respond to your children during an argument? In what ways is your response similar to or different from how your parents interacted with you?
4. What are some of your family traditions? What would you like to change about your celebrations this year?
5. Gandhi said, "There is more to life than increasing its speed." Is your life on the fast track? List some specific ways you can choose to slow down this year.

Chapter 12: "Oops, We Did It Again"

1. In what ways have you found it difficult to forgive yourself?
2. Is it difficult for you to ask your children for forgiveness? If so, why? How was forgiveness modeled in your home as you grew up?
3. In light of confessing your sins to others, have your children seen your brokenness and imperfections?
4. What role did truth telling have in your family of origin? Is it hard to tell or require truth in your new family? Why or why not?

Chapter 13: "But What If I Messed Up?"

1. What do you regret from your past that you hope your children will *never* have to experience?
2. Do you feel disqualified to teach proper choices to your children because of your past mistakes? Why or why not?
3. How has the "rating" of sins—from almost insignificant to barely forgivable—altered your perception of your own sins? Do you internally rank different sins—your own and those of others? If so, why?
4. Did your parents share cautionary tales with you? If so, recount one. What, if anything, prevents you from sharing age-appropriate cautionary tales with your children?

Chapter 14: "A Funny Thing Happened While Raising My Kids"

1. Did you grow up too fast because of your past? How has that affected the way you view life today?
2. When was the last time you had a belly laugh with your children? Do you feel that you need to open up more to fun, joy, and laughter?
3. Imagine today that laughter permeated your home. What would be different? In what ways would you be different?

Chapter 15: "Why Can't I Go to Grandpa's House?"

1. What would prevent you from allowing your child to visit a particular relative? List those reasons.
2. Write out a prayer of protection over your children, asking God to be with them in every situation. Ask him to protect their relationships with their grandparents. How did writing your prayer help you connect with God?
3. What limits or boundaries do you have in place when your children visit relatives?
4. What qualities do your parents have that you can praise in front of your children?
5. List three ways you can encourage a connection between your children and their grandparents this month. How would encouraging those connections differ from what you currently do?

Chapter 16: "Someone, Please Help Us!"

1. Do you have a mentor—another adult who speaks into your life? If so, who? If not, list the characteristics of the type of parenting mentor you'd like to have.
2. Spend this week "observing" people who parent well. Did you find any? What did the encounter(s) teach you about parenting?
3. If you don't have a parenting mentor, who could fill that role in your life today? Ask the Lord to guide you to the one(s) who will speak into your heart.
4. What questions would you eventually like a mentor to answer? What accountability questions would you like a mentor to ask you? List them.

Chapter 17: "I Can't Wipe the Wilderness Off My Shoes"

1. How does the truth that God will never leave you provide you with a source of help and strength today? How does this knowledge give you hope for the future?
2. What are your three biggest fears in raising your children? Read Genesis 26:24; Exodus 14:13; Joshua 10:25; Psalm 27:3; and Matthew 10:28. How do these verses help you face and understand your fears?
3. What stories from your childhood would you like to share with your children to illustrate how God rescued you?
4. Read Psalm 78:4-8. How does it invigorate you as a parent to know that the way you parent today will affect generation upon generation?

Chapter 18: "The Wolves Are Howling"

1. How does knowing that life is not fair affect the way you parent your children?
2. How did your parents view and handle money? In what ways do your money habits differ from theirs? What steps are you taking to teach your children about handling money responsibly?
3. Reread Adoniram Judson's letter to his fiancée's father. As a parent, how would you respond to such words?
4. How do your children differ from one another? How do you differ from your spouse? What are your children's spiritual gifts? How does knowing each child's uniqueness help you parent your children better?

Chapter 19: "We're in This Together"

1. Have you ever received a stinging rebuke about your parenting? From whom? How did it affect you then? In what ways, if any, do the words still affect you today?
2. Recount a time when you encouraged another parent and found yourself refreshed as a result.
3. Do you know other pioneer parents? List three specific ways you can encourage them this week.
4. Whom has God placed in your path that you might be able to mentor? What, if anything, is preventing you from mentoring this person?

Chapter 20: "What Now?"

1. In what ways does having an eternal perspective help you teach your children about life's inevitable sufferings?
2. What does worship look like in your family?
3. How does Paul's encouragement to make the most of your days change your view of how you parent today?
4. What specifically can you do to teach your children about heaven and the importance of having an eternal perspective?

Appendix

Helpful Resources

BOOKS

The Christian Life

Alcorn, Randy C. *Heaven*. Wheaton, IL: Tyndale, 2004. Anything Randy Alcorn writes, including his novels, is worth the read. This gift book summarizes his views on heaven and eternal perspective. Nothing has altered my view of life, healing, and parenting more than Alcorn's words.

Alcorn, Randy C. *Money, Possessions, and Eternity*. Wheaton, IL: Tyndale, 2003. An eye-opening, convicting book about the resources God entrusts to us. If you truly want to be a radical disciple of Jesus, and you want to lead your family in that same direction, read this book.

Bonhoeffer, Dietrich. *The Cost of Discipleship*. New York: Simon & Schuster, 1995. Bonhoeffer helps disciples understand the cost of following Jesus Christ.

Brother Lawrence. *The Practice of the Presence of God*. Peabody, MA: Hendrickson, 2004. I usually read this book once a year just to remind myself that God is ever present with me, even as I do dishes or labor in obscurity.

Crabb, Larry. *The Pressure's Off: There's a New Way to Live*. Colorado Springs: WaterBrook, 2002. A wonderful book for those who feel as if we have to follow formulas to be acceptable to God and to make life work.

Hession, Roy. *The Calvary Road*. Fort Washington, PA: Christian Literature Crusade, 1997. This is a book I read annually to remind myself that God uses broken people. The reason I ask my children for forgiveness is revealed in the chapters of this beautiful, convicting book.

Swenson, Richard A. *Margin: Restoring Emotional, Physical, Financial, and Time Reserves to Overloaded Lives.* Colorado Springs: NavPress, 1995. Swenson reveals how progress has hindered our lives as he demonstrates the necessity of adding margin—to live fuller lives without as much stress and angst.

Devotionals
Chambers, Oswald. *My Utmost for His Highest.* Uhrichsville, OH: Barbour, 2005. Although I've read this devotional for years, I still am deeply touched by Chambers's challenging words.

Cowman, L. B. *Streams in the Desert: 366 Daily Devotional Readings.* Grand Rapids: Zondervan, 1999. This devotional is like salve on a festering wound for those who suffer.

DeMuth, Mary E. *Ordinary Mom, Extraordinary God.* Eugene, OR: Harvest House, 2005. A shameless plug for my sixty-day devotional, in which I highlight God's strength in my own weakness. He is extraordinary; I am ordinary. How much we all need the extraordinary touch of Jesus.

Healing for the Past
Cloud, Henry. *Changes That Heal: How to Understand Your Past to Ensure a Healthier Future.* Grand Rapids: Zondervan, 1994. One of the most crucial books God used to reorient my thinking about him, my past, and how I live in the present.

Crabb, Larry. *Inside Out: Real Change Is Possible if You're Willing to Start from the Beginning.* Colorado Springs: NavPress, 1998. This book helped me grasp the importance of God healing me from the inside out.

Stoop, David A. and James Masteller. *Forgiving Our Parents, Forgiving Ourselves: Healing Adult Children of Dysfunctional Families.* Ventura, CA: Gospel Light, 2004. An amazing book that touches on all aspects of forgiveness, including the question of whether we can forgive and forget.

Tada, Joni Eareckson and Steve Estes. *When God Weeps: Why Our Sufferings Matter to the Almighty.* Grand Rapids: Zondervan, 1997. Joni gave me hope that my suffering in this present life matters to Jesus. She lifted my gaze above my present circumstances to consider the eternal impact my sufferings may have on the Kingdom of God.

Healing from Sexual Abuse

Allender, Dan B. *The Wounded Heart: Hope for Adult Victims of Childhood Sexual Abuse.* Colorado Springs: NavPress, 1990. This book helped uncover some destructive patterns I didn't even know I had. Be sure to purchase the accompanying workbook so you can adequately wade through all the issues.

Langberg, Diane Mandt. *On the Threshold of Hope: Opening the Door to Hope and Healing for Survivors of Sexual Abuse.* Wheaton, IL: Tyndale, 1999. Another great book for uncovering layers of pain that need healing.

Parenting

Burkett, Larry and Rick Osborne. *Financial Parenting: Showing Your Kids that Money Matters.* Chicago: Moody, 1999. A useful, hands-on guide to navigating money issues with your children from toddlerhood to teenhood. I highly recommend this book.

Campbell, Ross. *How to Really Love Your Child.* Colorado Springs: Cook, 2004. This book has been instrumental in helping me connect deeply with my children. When I sense myself straying, I reread it.

Cline, Foster W. and Jim Fay. *Parenting with Love and Logic: Teaching Children Responsibility.* Colorado Springs: Pinon Press, 1990. One of the most practical, joyful ways of parenting I've found. The authors teach how to empathize with our children while allowing real-life consequences to teach them.

Dobson, James C. *The New Dare to Discipline.* Wheaton, IL: Tyndale, 1996. This is the first parenting book I ever read. Full of practical and biblically sound advice, this volume should be on every parent's bookshelf.

Hunt, Gladys M. *Honey for a Child's Heart: The Imaginative Use of Books in Family Life.* Grand Rapids: Zondervan, 2002. A terrific book about the importance of reading and telling stories to your children. Once you read this, you'll want to cozy up to your children and open a classic.

Kimmel, Tim. *Grace-Based Parenting: Set Your Family Free.* Nashville: W Publishing, 2005. A balanced and freeing book about infusing grace (in place of legalism and control) into your home.

Leman, Kevin. *Making Children Mind Without Losing Yours.* Grand Rapids: Revell, 2005. A hilarious but true read. I love the way Leman echoes Love and Logic strategies with humor and candor.

Pipher, Mary. *The Shelter of Each Other: Rebuilding Our Families.* New York: Ballantine, 1997. An interesting sociological book about families. I love Pipher's emphasis on getting our families outdoors to reconnect. This is not a Christian book, but it is an inspiring one nonetheless.

Rainey, Dennis and Barbara Rainey. *Parenting Today's Adolescent: Helping Your Child Avoid the Traps of the Preteen and Teen Years.* With Bruce Nygren. Nashville: Thomas Nelson, 2002. This book comes highly recommended by friends who work for FamilyLife Ministries.

Tripp, Tedd. *Shepherding a Child's Heart.* Wapwallopen, PA: Shepherd, 1998. A lovely approach to parenting our children as a shepherd would take care of his sheep. Tripp delves into heart issues, challenging parents to love their children well.

FAMILY WEB SITES

www.familylife.com—FamilyLife's main ministry page. Register for the life-changing marriage conferences, "A Weekend to Remember," or the one-day seminars, "I Still Do." The site also features resources and information about the ministry's daily radio broadcasts.

www.family.org—Focus on the Family's main site. Find resources, CDs, books, and other family-related products.

www.loveandlogic.com—A terrific site to find Love and Logic books and tapes. Do yourself a favor and purchase a tape. You'll be entertained as well as enlightened. One of the best parenting systems available.

Notes

Preface

1. For more on Robin Warren and Barry Marshall's ulcer research, see Richard Currey, "Barry Marshall: Persistence Paid Off," October 15, 1998, http://science-education.nih.gov/Snapshots.nsf/story?openForm& rtn~SB_Hpylori_Marshall.

Chapter 1

1. Don Frank and Jan Frank, *Unclaimed Baggage: Dealing with the Past on Your Way to a Stronger Marriage* (Colorado Springs: NavPress, 2003), 22.

Chapter 2

1. Don Frank and Jan Frank, *Unclaimed Baggage: Dealing with the Past on Your Way to a Stronger Marriage* (Colorado Springs: NavPress, 2003), 47.
2. See 2 Corinthians 5:17.

Chapter 3

1. For the whole story, see John 5:1-9.
2. For the whole story, see Mark 8:22-26.
3. L. B. Cowman, *Streams in the Desert: 366 Daily Devotional Readings* (Grand Rapids: Zondervan, 1997), 41.
4. For the whole story, see John 4:6-42.

Chapter 4

1. Steven Curtis Chapman and Scotty Smith, *Speechless: Living in Awe of God's Disruptive Grace* (Grand Rapids: Zondervan, 2000), 104-5.
2. If you can't seem to get beyond the vows you have made or if your heart wants to remain walled off due to fear, consider visiting a licensed

Christian counselor. I spent two years in counseling to work through issues of my past. Sometimes it's difficult to find just the right counselor for you. For suggestions on finding a counselor that fits, see http://www.finders-seekers.com/articles/article10.php.

Chapter 5

1. Dietrich Bonhoeffer, *The Cost of Discipleship* (New York: Macmillan, 1937), 100.

Chapter 6

1. Don Frank and Jan Frank, *Unclaimed Baggage: Dealing with the Past on Your Way to a Stronger Marriage* (Colorado Springs: NavPress, 2003), 154.
2. Statement made during a presentation at a FamilyLife Marriage Conference, May 1998.

Chapter 7

1. Ben-Sira, quoted in Gerald Blidstein, *Honor Thy Father and Mother: Filial Responsibility in Jewish Law and Ethics* (New York: Ktav, 1976), 11.
2. Philo, quoted in Shaye J. D. Cohen, ed., *The Jewish Family in Antiquity* (Providence, RI: Brown University Press, 1993), 81.
3. Blidstein, *Honor Thy Father and Mother,* 131.
4. Oswald Chambers, *My Utmost for His Highest* (Westwood, NJ: Barbour and Company, 1935), 11.
5. Dietrich Bonhoeffer, *The Cost of Discipleship* (New York: Macmillan, 1937), 99.

Chapter 8

1. For more on this idea, see Larry Crabb, *The Pressure's Off: There's a New Way to Live* (Colorado Springs: WaterBrook, 2002), 12.
2. Roy Hession, *The Calvary Road* (Fort Washington, PA: Christian Literature Crusade, 1950), 13-14.
3. Oswald Chambers, *My Utmost for His Highest* (Westwood, NJ: Barbour and Company, 1935), 126.

Chapter 9

1. Dietrich Bonhoeffer, *The Cost of Discipleship* (New York: Macmillan, 1937), 66.
2. Bonhoeffer, *Cost of Discipleship*, 99.

Chapter 10

1. L. B. Cowman, *Streams in the Desert: 366 Daily Devotional Readings* (Grand Rapids: Zondervan, 1997), 182.

Chapter 11

1. Ross Campbell, *How to Really Love Your Child* (Colorado Springs: Chariot Victor, 1992), 31.
2. Campbell, *How to Really Love Your Child*, 34.
3. Oswald Chambers, *My Utmost for His Highest* (Westwood, NJ: Barbour and Company, 1935), 121.
4. Gladys M. Hunt, *Honey for a Child's Heart: The Imaginative Use of Books in Family Life* (Grand Rapids: Zondervan, 1989), 14.
5. The Bible is replete with verses singing its praise. It is "living and active. Sharper than any double-edged sword, it penetrates even to dividing soul and spirit, joints and marrow; it judges the thoughts and attitudes of the heart" (Hebrews 4:12). "All Scripture is God-breathed and is useful for teaching, rebuking, correcting and training in righteousness, so that the man of God may be thoroughly equipped for every good work" (2 Timothy 3:16-17).
6. William Makepeace Thackeray, quoted in Leonard Roy Frank, *Random House Webster's Quotationary* (New York: Random House, 2001), 436.
7. Jack S. Deere, *Surprised by the Voice of God* (Grand Rapids: Zondervan, 1996), 319.
8. Richard A. Swenson, *Margin: Restoring Emotional, Physical, Financial and Time Reserves to Overloaded Lives* (Colorado Springs: NavPress, 1992), 91-92.
9. Mary Pipher, *The Shelter of Each Other: Rebuilding Our Families* (New York: Ballantine Books, 1996), 263.

Chapter 13

1. An excellent book that highlights this principle is *Wisdom and the Millers: Proverbs for Children* by Mildred A. Martin (Mifflin, PA: Green Pastures Press, 1993).

Chapter 14

1. Dean Mobbs et al., "Humor Modulates the Mesolimbic Reward Centers," *Neuron* 40, no. 5 (2003): 1041-48.
2. Mark Twain, quoted in Leonard Roy Frank, *Random House Webster's Quotationary* (New York: Random House, 2001), 436.
3. See Keith C. Heidorn, "Laugh Away Stress," *Living Gently Quarterly* (2001). http://members.shaw.ca/keithheidorn/lgqarticles/laugh.htm.

Chapter 15

1. Sometimes it's impossible to reconcile with your parents. Or perhaps you've experienced the numbing loss of one or both of your parents. In either case, you can still preserve a grandparent-like relationship for your children. Begin to ask the Lord to bring in grandparent-types from the body of Christ to fill that need in your children. We live two thousand miles away from grandparents, so my children don't get a lot of time with them. God answered our prayer by blessing our children with Jack and Helen, who joyfully act as surrogate grandparents.

Chapter 16

1. Contact information for the parachurch organizations listed in text is as follows: FamilyLife: www.familylife.com, 800-358-6329; Focus on the Family: www.family.org, 800-232-6459; Hearts at Home: www.hearts-at-home.org, 309-888-6667; MOPS (Mothers of Preschoolers): www.gospelcom.net/mops, 303-733-5353; Moms in Touch: www.momsintouch.org, 800-949-6667.

Chapter 17

1. Walter Wangerin Jr., "Making Disciples by Sacred Story," *Christianity Today* 48, no. 2 (February 2004): 68.

Chapter 18

1. H. Norman Wright, *Family Is Still a Great Idea* (Ann Arbor: Servant, 1992), 243.
2. Quoted in L. B. Cowman, *Streams in the Desert: 366 Daily Devotional Readings* (Grand Rapids: Zondervan, 1997), 24.
3. Adoniram Judson, quoted in "Devoted for Life: The Life and Death of Adoniram Judson," Precept Ministries International, http://preceptaustin .org/Adoniram_Judson.htm.
4. Letter to Sophie, December 24, 2003. See Mary DeMuth, *Ordinary Mom, Extraordinary God* (Eugene, OR: Harvest House, 2005), 103-4.
5. Randy Alcorn, quoted in "Christian Book Distributors Interview with Randy Alcorn," Eternal Perspective Ministries, www.epm.org/articles/ cbdint.html.

Chapter 20

1. Randy Alcorn, *In Light of Eternity: Perspectives on Heaven* (Colorado Springs: WaterBrook(Grand Rapids: Zondervan, 1997), 211.
2. Joni Eareckson Tada and Steven Estes, *When God Weeps: Why Our Sufferings Matter to the Almighty* (Grand Rapids: Zondervan, 1997), 211.
3. Randy Alcorn, "About EPM: Heartbeat of EPM," Eternal Perspective Ministries, www.epm.org/heartbeat.html.